The

REALLY USEFUL
DRAMA BOOK

The Really Useful Drama Book offers busy primary school teachers a collection of step-by-step drama sessions, inspired by high-quality picturebooks, that will engage children and promote enjoyable learning across the curriculum.

Lively and thoughtful, the interactive drama sessions are structured around a wide range of texts, including wordless picturebooks, postmodern picturebooks, short stories, well-known texts by recognisable authors and some you may not have come across before, all chosen for their power to foster curiosity. The step-by-step sessions can also be adapted to incorporate your own ideas and passions, allowing you to structure them for the topics you're exploring with your class.

Each session is structured around two texts and offers a guide to the drama strategies used, teaching objectives, ideas for writing opportunities, problems, emotions and challenges to explore, and a clear guide to exploring each text. Ten key themes are explored:

- Suspense
- Prejudice
- Friendship
- Rhyme and rhythm
- War and conflict
- Nature
- Overcoming fear
- Possessions and obsessions
- Dreams
- Short stories

With a focus on the crucial role of imagination in the classroom, *The Really Useful Drama Book* helps reclaim a purposeful, passionate pedagogy and shows teachers how drama can place children right at the heart of a story, encouraging their desire to ask questions, solve problems and search out new information.

Roger McDonald is Senior Lecturer in Primary Education at the University of Greenwich, UK.

The Really Useful Series

The

REALLY USEFUL DRAMA BOOK

Using Picturebooks to Inspire Imaginative Learning

Roger McDonald

Routledge
Taylor & Francis Group

LONDON AND NEW YORK

First published 2017
by Routledge
2 Park Square, Milton Park, Abingdon, Oxon OX14 4RN

and by Routledge
711 Third Avenue, New York, NY 10017

Routledge is an imprint of the Taylor & Francis Group, an informa business

British Library Cataloguing-in-Publication Data
A catalogue record for this book is available from the British Library

Library of Congress Cataloging-in-Publication Data
A catalog record for this book has been requested

ISBN: 978-1-138-18599-9 (hbk)
ISBN: 978-1-138-18601-9 (pbk)
ISBN: 978-1-315-64411-0 (ebk)

Typeset in Palatino and Gill Sans
by Florence Production Ltd, Stoodleigh, Devon, UK

To Mop and Pop x

Contents

Acknowledgements

I would like to thank all the children, staff, parents, students and teachers I have worked with who have supported me in developing imaginative ideas in the classroom, in particular the head teachers I have worked with: Ray Morris, Lynn Andrews and Janice Kingman, whose relentless commitment to nurture, develop and value every child, regardless of ability or background, has been truly inspirational. In addition thanks to a wonderful teacher, Karen Crossley, who teaches with passion and purpose and is always willing to try out ideas and offer advice.

Special thanks to Professor Andrew Lambirth, University of Greenwich, Professor Teresa Cremin, Open University, and Professor Kathy Goouch, Canterbury Christ Church University, who first introduced me to the power of imaginative engagement with texts and have been a source of encouragement and support over the years.

In addition I would like to thank Laura Braun from Petworth C of E Primary School, West Sussex for the permission to publish work created by the children in Maple Class.

Introduction

I can remember as a student teacher being totally captivated by a workshop I attended. It was a drama workshop led by Teresa Cremin who, at the time, worked at Canterbury Christ Church University where I was a student. I must admit that the prospect of attending a drama workshop as part of my studies did not fill me with a great deal of excitement. My mind turned to the drama I experienced in secondary school where once a week we went to a dedicated studio in order to respond to a piece of music or prose. My recollections of involvement in secondary drama involved going through the motions in order to please the teacher with the aim of getting out to lunch on time. As far as primary school is concerned I only remember the end of term school plays which we performed for our parents.

It was therefore with slight trepidation and nervousness that I followed the signs to the drama workshop at university. The first thing that struck me was that it was taking place in one of the regular classrooms. My preconceptions meant that I assumed it would be in the hall or an area where all the tables and chairs would have been removed to provide space for 'the drama'. The second thing I noticed was the display of texts on a table at the front of the classroom. I had been introduced to so many stories over the course and had started building my own collection of picturebooks as well as novels for my own teaching, so seeing that there may be a link with the drama session did serve to ease some of my nervousness.

The session did indeed start with a story and before I knew it I was taking part in a range of drama conventions resulting in me gradually gaining a deeper understanding of the people, places and predicaments within the text. The difference was the authenticity of what we were doing. Within the text there were problems to solve which we wanted, indeed felt compelled, to solve. I was drawn into the lives of the characters in the text in a way that I had not previously experienced. I can honestly say that I had never felt this connection with a text before. This feeling was due to the power of the emotional connection facilitated through the drama. The session drastically changed my perceptions of what drama was and how it can place you, not on the periphery of a story, but right at the heart of the story, making decisions and asking questions which will affect the journey the story takes.

There was a true purpose which was put across with passion leading to me feeling empowered. This was something I wanted to make a hallmark of my teaching. It was imperative for children in my class *to feel* something about the stories we shared rather than going through the motions as I had done. Twenty years on from that workshop my classes and I have experienced a range of predicaments through drama. These have included the need to save our ship which was most surely going to be destroyed in the storm, we have walked along the menacing corridor after experiencing our first nightmare, we ran home after being lost for days, read the letter which we had kept sealed for all those years, stood with our granddad at the graveside – reflecting, protested outside the council chambers and saved our village from the destruction of the beast.

In my early career a number of issues resonated with me. The most important has been the recognition of a need for an emotional connection in the work that we do. Both teachers and children need to feel something which connects them with the work. This drives the need and desire to ask questions, solve problems and search out new information. Also it was evident that authenticity was essential. There needs to be an authentic reason to invest in the work. Using drama strategies often creates a suitable vehicle for this. In addition the development of the imagination is crucial as it has the power to create possibilities in the mind of the learner. Finally the need for the teacher and children to be collaborative learners together serves to adjust the power balance in the classroom and enables authentic learning to take place. Since then I have explored these areas as part of my work with children, students and teachers highlighting the necessity for teaching to be characterised by passion and purpose for empowerment. There are however some potential barriers to this which will also be addressed in this book.

The first section in this book explores the issue of imaginative engagement. It looks first at the current educational landscape noting the dangers of a shifting pedagogy towards a standards-led agenda. An argument is made that the shifting pedagogy can be to the detriment of imaginative teaching and learning. Then we will turn our attention to how we can reclaim an imaginative pedagogy and what teaching with purpose and passion for empowerment actually means and looks like. Imagination will then be defined before focusing on teaching imaginatively through process drama.

The second section incorporates all of these elements and exemplifies how imaginative learning can be created across the curriculum through the use of interactive strategies, including drama, which open up possibilities to a world of creation, speculation and reflection. This section incorporates 10 themes which can be used and adapted. Within each theme two texts exemplify how interactive imaginative strategies can help deepen children's understanding. A wide range of texts have been chosen including wordless picturebooks, postmodern picturebooks, short stories, well-known texts by recognisable authors and some texts which may be less familiar to the reader. Some texts will be easily assessable whereas others, such as *The Kraken*, may need to be specifically ordered. This is intentional as curiosity can be built with the class by getting hold of a copy of a book which may be less well known.

How to use this book

If you are reading this book it is likely that you are a student, a classroom teacher, a senior leader or a teaching assistant working within a school. You therefore already have a wealth of experience to draw on. You also will have had or be experiencing training which will encourage you to be reflective and question the practice you see as well as partake in. In addition it is possible that you may at times feel pressured: pressured to ensure you show evidence of progress, pressured to identify and explain the progress of your children and pressured to follow and adopt the latest initiative from university, the local authority, the academy chain or trust.

This pressure can sometimes result in a shift in our pedagogy in order to follow what is deemed to be *good practice*. This book asks you to take time to reflect on your own practice, to identify the elements which are informed by research and to question practice which may inevitably have found its way into our teaching but, when given time to reflect, we are unable to justify. In addition this book aims to support you with ideas for developing or possibly repositioning yourself as a creative teacher fostering the imaginative experiences of the children within your class.

It is important to note therefore that this book is not a 'how to' guide or a scheme with ideas to follow rigidly. It celebrates and appreciates the experience every professional teacher holds and encourages you to weave as many of the ideas as you see fit within your current teaching. Every teacher is different and every classroom unique. Therefore every time ideas within this book are used they should also be different. You will adapt and shape the ideas depending on your own personality, experience and interests as well as that of your classes. What works well in one class in one year may not in another.

There are ten themes within the book chosen so that they can be adapted to complement some of the topics you may be covering. You will easily identify links between the themes as well and may want to interchange some of the chosen texts. Within each theme two texts have been chosen with a range of interactive ideas for you to use in the classroom. It is intended, indeed expected, that these will be moulded by yourself and will serve to complement the work you are already undertaking.

You will see examples of work from children included in some of the chapters. Often this is work which children have completed in the flow of the drama rather than work which has been edited and presented formally. Each child will have experienced something slightly different, approached the drama from their own perspective and been affected by different feelings in the midst of the drama. In many cases the work will reflect this raw process before any intervention from the teacher.

For those who are new to using drama strategies within the classroom then you may want to experiment by choosing one of the texts outlined. Choose one that you know or one of the themes which appeals to you. Use the ideas presented to develop your own planning and aim to incorporate two or three of the drama strategies. Focus on your ability to question, create productive tension, predict and lead discussions within the drama rather than following a set plan. Know what you hope the general outcome will be. You may want children to find out more about a particular location, develop question skills or identify with a character within a text. There are suggestions for objectives at the start of each text.

However you choose to use the ideas in this book, enjoy playing with the possibilities, entering new worlds and triggering the emotional connection of imaginative ideas through drama.

PART I

Introduction

1 The changing educational landscape

A SHIFTING PEDAGOGY

In the busy world of teaching we can sometimes get swept away with the latest educational trend telling us what '*good practice*' is. Over the last 20 years a range of initiatives have influenced the way we have taught. These have been government-based initiatives such as the National Literacy Strategy and the Primary Strategies, Local Authority-led initiatives as well as school-led initiatives. All of these affect our pedagogy and therefore impact on the children within our classes. However do we analyse where these initiatives originate from? Do we consider whether they are based in rigorous, relevant and current research and do we evaluate whether they are suitable for our classroom or school setting? Whatever the latest initiative is, the phrase which often gets espoused is 'we are doing this in order to *drive up standards*'. It is worth taking a moment to explore this in more detail.

Understandably the need to raise standards seems to be a general mantra from head teachers, senior school leaders and class teachers. In fact the 'drive to raise standards' (Alexander, 2010 p. 1) has formed a central element of recent education policy in England. This has resulted in the proliferation of the 'performance' agenda within schools which in turn has heightened the tension between what Cox (2011) notes as the market-driven systems and an understanding that children are 'active meaning makers' (Cox, 2011 p. 37).

It is interesting therefore to consider and explore whether this performance agenda has influenced teaching within the classroom and the culture adopted by schools. Have teachers and schools inadvertently shifted their pedagogy? One factor possibly affecting the shifting pedagogy is the perceived pressure felt by teachers as a result of the increased accountability. Indeed Alexander (2010) notes that in many primary schools 'a professional culture of excitement, inventiveness and healthy scepticism has been supplanted by one of dependency, compliance and even fear' (p. 7).

THE PERFORMANCE AGENDA

It could be argued that the performance agenda has led to an expansion of an objectives-led orthodoxy in primary schools with a focus on educational outcomes rather than educational processes. Take a moment to think about your own classroom and the pedagogy adopted. Can you articulate the pedagogy adopted? Do you know whether it is research based? Is it an autonomous or ideological approach? In some schools teachers experience a culture which relates to an objective-led curriculum. In these schools for each lesson children are told the objective, given a set of success criteria and their work is marked specifically against the set criteria. The danger with this approach is that the curriculum can become objective led rather than learning led.

This approach focuses on the minutiae of the objectives due to the need to prove and measure progress but can lose sight of the importance of creating desire, curiosity and intrigue in the work presented to the children. The use of objectives in this way suggests that learning can be predicted. A teacher can plan a sequence of lessons or learning steps and be certain of the outcome for each child in the class. This process does not take into account the imaginative or creative elements which, by their very nature, are unpredictable (Cox, 2011) and instead believes that measures can be made of progress and therefore of teacher effectiveness (Cox, 2011).

PERFORMANCE GOALS

The shift towards an objective-led, formulaic, structured and criteria-based learning experience identified in some schools results in an increased focus on performance. This can have devastating effects on creativity and the imagination. Dweck (1988) explains how the pressured learning experience and externally driven performance goals can lead to a decline in risk taking resulting in creativity diminishing (Burke, 2011). Therefore the implications of this approach impact on both the teacher, who increasingly looks to be told what and how to teach, and the child, who increasingly seeks reassurance that they are reaching their potential (whatever that may be).

Performance goals are externally driven and are apparent where the child feels the need to 'document or gain favourable judgements of their competency' (Burke, 2011 p. 19). These goals focus on 'the adequacy of their ability' (Dweck, 1988 p. 6) and can result in the child feeling vulnerable in their learning leading to 'the helpless response in the face of failure, setting up low ability attributions, negative affect and impaired performance' (Dweck, 1988 p. 6). Parallels could be drawn between the definition of performance goals and the pedagogy in the classroom; the use of objectives, success criteria, individual targets and formulaic writing techniques where children are given sets of 'ambitious' vocabulary, sentence openers, punctuation and connectives to structure their writing. These approaches are mainly concerned with measuring ability.

Indeed it is interesting to examine the effects of performance goals as identified by Dweck (1988) and consider whether these are prevalent in classrooms across England. She notes five cognitive and affective factors associated with performance goals. The first is a loss of self-belief and in the utility of effort. The second effect sees a withdrawal of effort due to the belief that continued effort will 'further document low ability' (Dweck, 1988 p. 7). The third effect is the focus on the goal itself at the expense of the learning. Fourth the child may exhibit signs of anxiety or shame which in turn motivate them to try to escape the task or learning. The last effect is the barrier which is put up to intrinsic rewards due to a concern over a possible negative judgement.

You may be able to identify with this pedagogy as it not only affects the children but also the teachers. The process of focusing on the performance of children has inevitably led to the measuring of teacher's performance. The pressure, accountability and performance-generated goals for both teachers and children have therefore led to a move towards the adoption of a form of measuring process to indicate progression. This allows a class teacher, year group leader and ultimately the head teacher to demonstrate the progress which has been made by both children and teachers leading ultimately to the 'raising of standards'.

MEASURING PROGRESS

The measurement tool for assessing literacy can originate from a number of sources. Assessing Pupil Progress materials are still available and used by a number of schools. Also a range of end of key stage descriptors were recently published by the Department for Education, with evidence suggesting that they have been adopted and adapted by some schools. In addition there are a number of schemes available which can be adopted. Indeed one increasingly popular resource published by Andrell Education is called 'Big Writing'. This resource comes complete with an assessment tool in the form of a criterion scale which it is believed can demonstrate progress in writing.

Many schools in South East England have adopted the 'Big Writing' scheme (Barrett, 2014) which is based on the work of Ros Wilson (2002) with the aim of raising writing scores by the end of Key Stage Two. By adopting the teaching techniques children are expected to make progress by learning how to use the features of VCOP (vocabulary, connectives, openers and punctuation) in their writing and in turn are able to up-level their sentences. However as Cremin and Myhill (2011) note, this widespread approach is 'little more than an incremental process of skill acquisition, which fails to recognise the role of reading, of texts and of literature in particular as a rich source of imaginative possibilities for writing' (p. 60). To me there can be no doubt that the principles of this resource, if used how the publishers recommend, can support the work in the classroom. However the danger here is that if we abandon our principles, disregard research and follow a formulaic, mechanistic and structured approach to teaching literacy it will inevitably be in opposition to what Alexander (2009) argues for, which is a pedagogy of repertoire and principle as opposed to one of recipe and prescription.

It could be argued that I have painted a bleak picture of the educational landscape at the current time. I do not necessarily see it like that. In contrast to performance goals we can turn our attention to learning goals. Learning goals are internally driven and are concerned with the individual's desire to increase their own learning, understanding and skill development (Burke, 2011; Dweck, 1988). In this situation the child, who may indeed have low opinions of their current ability, will adopt a distinctive attitude towards learning because, as Dweck (1988) notes, '(a) they are not focused on judgements of their current abilities, (b) errors are not as indicative of goal failure within a learning goal and, (c) low current ability in a valued area may make skill acquisition even more desirable' (p. 6). It is on the need to readdress the balance towards learning rather than performance that this book will focus.

There have always been challenges in education and conflicts between political needs and educational ones. However, the dedication and hard work from teachers in the classroom on a daily basis who resist the specific shift in pedagogy noted here and the determination of leaders charting the school's direction through the educational landscape are testament to what can be achieved. Therefore, as long as we recognise current and relevant research, we are in safe hands. These are the teachers and school leaders who recognise the importance of teaching with passion and purpose.

TEACHING WITH PURPOSE, PASSION AND EMPOWERMENT

You may remember, as a teacher or as a child, the summer term ritual where the whole school sits expectantly in the school hall while the classes for the year ahead are read out. Children look around the hall with beady eyes and a sense of anticipation as each class is read out with the name of the new teacher. From the children's point of view they know which teacher they want and are ready to erupt with a choral 'yeeessss!' if the teacher's name matches their class. Also from the teachers' point of view they wait with the same anticipation to see what the reaction will be from the children when the head teacher reveals the classes and the teachers for the year ahead.

I wonder what it is that causes the resounding 'yessss' or conversely what it is which means that a teacher's name would be met simply with quiet acceptance? Maybe the children have built perceptions of each teacher, looking at how they operate around the school, listening to their friends and noting the degree of 'fun' emanating from their classrooms. Of course there may be many other reasons for children to want to be taught by a particular teacher. However, for the anticipation and expectation to be borne out as meaningful and lasting I would argue that the teacher would need to display passion in their teaching and for their care of the children, a clear joint purpose in what they are doing which takes the children's individual needs into consideration and the understanding that they are empowering the children to make choices for themselves.

In essence children are possibly looking for teachers who respond to them as children, who adapt the plans for them and create excitement and curiosity within the lessons. Children and teachers will be learning together, finding out and discovering new things and bringing their own backgrounds and perspectives to bear on the work they are doing. Children, I would argue, are looking for teachers who reject the shifting pedagogy and instead focus on something more important than the performance-focused goals referred to earlier. They are looking for teachers who are themselves excited about education, motivated by learning and creators of intrigue and curiosity.

This is highlighted in Ken Robinson's (2013) excellent TED talk entitled 'How to escape education's death valley'. Ken talks about the importance of the role of a teacher in not just teaching but in educating children. He makes the comparison between the practice of 'teaching' and the practice of 'dieting' noting that you could be involved in dieting without losing any weight and likewise could be involved in teaching without children learning anything! He equates this with the delivery system of education which, it could be argued, has penetrated our teaching through the various schemes schools adopt.

It is not, in my view, the schemes which are necessarily the problem but the way in which they are adopted by schools. For example one academy trust with over thirty-five schools has adopted schemes for both Maths and English with the expectation that teachers follow the scheme exactly in order to ensure a similar 'rate of progress' across the year groups. It may be helpful to briefly look at the history of the pedagogy which has built up around such planning frameworks. These schemes or planning frameworks are mostly derived from Tyler's rationale (1949) which, in turn, is based on the principles of John Dewey. The schemes and lesson plans follow a familiar formula often beginning with statements of objectives for the lesson or unit, followed by a selection of content that will meet the objectives, and finally some means of evaluating whether the objectives have indeed been met. Egan (1992) notes that while Tyler's work, drawing on Dewey, is 'clearly hospitable to imaginative activity, the system-atizing of his framework over the past 40 years or so has fallen increasingly into the hands of people who have aimed at a desiccated sense of efficiency and have favoured a more behaviourist approach' (Egan, 1992 p. 91). So here we can see an example of taking a principle of education which is sound but which through applying the pressure of accountability the principle morphs into something which resembles some of the original characteristics but has a completely different effect and outcome.

In this delivery mode of education children are seen as vessels to be filled with information rather than giving the opportunity to experience an education which responds to the individual needs of the child and also understands the differing characteristics of the teachers in the classes. Why is it that Mr Whatsit in Class 4W should be teaching in the same way or indeed the same subject matter as Mrs Noggins in Class 4N? Of course busy teachers or school leaders will turn to schemes to help with planning. This is a sensible and logical option as long as the teachers are given the autonomy to change, adapt, amend and sometimes ditch the set planning in response to their own and their children's needs and interests.

Therefore, as educators, we need to be aware of the dangers of a scheme-led, uniform and formalistic curriculum approach by ensuring that the elements of teaching with purpose, passion and empowerment are explicit within our teaching. We should question our school leaders when decisions are made regarding the curriculum. They should be able to justify their position based on a clear pedagogy which is based on an understanding of child development not purely on a desire to 'raise standards', whatever that may mean. One of the key elements within a curriculum which is purposeful and taught with passion is the need for the imagination to be valued and developed.

REFERENCES

Alexander, R. (2009). *Children, their World, their education: final report and recommendations of the Cambridge primary review*. London: Routledge.

Alexander, R. (2010). The perils of policy: success, amnesia and collateral damage in systematic educational reform. National Institute of Education, Singapore. The C.J.Koh Lecture Thursday 18th March 2010.

Barrett, S. (2014). Empowering young writers. In V. Bower (ed.), *Developing early literacy 0 to 8: from theory to practice* (pp. 184–99). London: Sage.

Burke, W. (2011). Log jammed by standard assessment tests: how feedback can help writers. *Literacy, 45*(1), 19–24.

Cremin, T., & Myhill, D. (2011). *Writing voices: creating communities of writers*. London: Routledge.

Cox, S. (2011). *New perspectives in primary education: meaning and purpose in learning and teaching*. Maidenhead: Oxford University Press.

Dewey, J. (1966) *Democracy and education*. New York: Free Press (first published 1916).

Dweck, C. (1988). Goals: an approach to motivation and achievement. *Journal of Personality and Social Psychology, 54*(1), 5–12.

Egan, K. (1992). *Imagination in teaching and learning: the middle school years*. Chicago: University of Chicago Press.

Robinson, K. (2013). How to escape education's death valley. Video retrieved from: www.ted.com/talks/ken_robinson_how_to_escape_education_s_death_valley?language=en

Tyler, R. (1949). *Basic principles of curriculum and instruction*. Chicago: University of Chicago Press.

Wilson, R. (2002) *Raising Standards in Writing: Strategies for immediate impact on writing standards*. Wakefield: Andrell Education.

2 Reclaiming the purpose and passion

IMAGINATION: THE ESSENTIAL ELEMENT

> I have also come very strongly to believe that it is the cultivation of imagination which should be the chief aim of education, and in which our present systems of education most conspicuously fail, where they do fail.
>
> (Warnock, 1976 p. 9)

The quote from Mary Warnock comes from her influential book on imagination which, although published nearly 40 years ago, is still one of the seminal texts in the field. We can surmise from the quote that there has been a continual battle for the imagination within the education system. We have already alluded to the pressure the educational system can put on teachers through terms such as 'good practice' which overlook the complexities of the teaching process (Lefstein and Snell, 2014). However within a classroom which values the imagination we know that teaching can be a messy process where we make hundreds of split-second decisions on an ongoing basis which influence the direction of the lesson and therefore the learning.

The imagination is a term which is used in our everyday conversations. You may hear people talking about children either not having any imagination or some children letting their imagination 'run away with them'. But what is the imagination? Is it something we value in school? Do we actively encourage its growth and development through our teaching in the classroom? Here we will look at the imagination, work towards a definition and identify its central place in teaching with interactive strategies such as drama.

The notion of imagination encompasses a range of meanings which have built up over time. The imagination has received a lot of attention from philosophers and academics which has led to our current understanding of the term. Indeed in ancient and medieval times it was considered that the imagination was actually trespassing on the powers which belonged to God (Egan, 1992).

Throughout this period the imagination or 'yester' which is the Hebrew name originating from 'yetsirah', which is translated as 'creation', was considered a dangerous capacity. Egan (1992) notes that it was 'inescapably bound up with attempts to usurp God's creative power' and that 'human creativity, that product of the active imagination, is seen constantly threatening to divide God from His people' (Egan, 1992 p. 13). So the imagination represented a rebellion against the status quo and political order because it empowered people to think in alternate ways to that which was expected.

DEFINING IMAGINATION

Let us first work towards a definition of imagination before looking at how it can be applied to our work in the classroom. Alphen (2011) defines imagination as 'a heightened form of cognition, capable of transforming the knowledge and skills to be learned into enhanced experiences. These experiences stimulate creativity in thinking and involve the emotions of the learners, through which a more meaningful relationship is established with the learning material' (Alphen, 2011 p. 16). This is an interesting definition as it draws on the ability to be creative and also the importance of the emotions of the learner. The sense that we 'feel' something through the use of the imagination is important and connects with the passion and purpose already alluded to. A simpler, well shorter, definition comes from Egan (2005) who defines imagination as 'the ability to think of things as possible – the source of flexibility and originality in human thinking' (Egan, 2005 p. 220). I don't think we would argue with these definitions. The values they highlight are admirable and ones which we know are important. The issue for some will be how these attributes 'fit' in with the curriculum set.

We can look at this in more detail with the help of Alphen (2011 p. 17) who expands on his definition with the following attributes of imagination:

* Imagination is the ability to picture something in the mind that bears a relationship to a phenomenon from the physical world or other human experience such as the psychological, mythical, spiritual or philosophical.

* All human endeavours to understand the universe and our lives require the activity of the imagination, a process of thinking in which we create images that 'picture' the phenomena that confront us.

* Imagination is able to go beyond the limitations of physical objects, stereotyped thinking, literal concepts, and is open to exploring associations, the development of ideas, broader formulations of concepts, perceiving deeper and richer meanings, creating original artefacts and probably a host of other activities that constitute human endeavour.

One of the key concepts for me is the development of curiosity. If we look at the definitions from Egan and Alphen they allude to the need for the learners to become curious about their learning, to ask questions and to generate new knowledge which is set within an authentic framework. The question for teachers is how can this be applied in the classroom?

IMAGINATION IN THE CLASSROOM

So how is this applicable to our work in the classroom and how does it relate to the use of drama conventions explored through high-quality picturebooks and short novels? If we base our definition of imagination on Egan's work and then look at his extended definition of imagination we can start to make clear links between the creative nature of the imagination and our work within the classroom. Egan noted that 'imagination is the capacity to think of things as possibly being so; it is an intentional act of mind; it is the source of invention, novelty, and generativity; it is not implicated in all perception and in the construction of all meaning; it is not distinct from rationality but is rather a capacity that greatly enriches rational thinking (Egan, 1992 p. 43). As educators we would surely subscribe to the desire to enrich our children's ability to think rationally, to consider possibilities rather than a culture of accepting what is given, and in turn to use this knowledge within not only the work they are doing but in their lives as a whole.

Through adopting an imaginative approach we give children the opportunity and, in a sense the permission, to think freely without the constraints of following a set lesson formula with specific objectives and success criteria which, used within the performance agenda, could have the effect of overlooking and not valuing individual ideas, thoughts and perception. This approach may sound straightforward but it often takes a shift in the teacher's and sometimes the children's perception of the perceived power relations in the classroom. As McKernan (2008) notes, 'by allowing students the opportunity to think freely for themselves we shed our being in authority and give this as a right to the student. This is what is emancipatory about education; it frees the student from the patria potestas, or the parental jurisdiction' (p. 23).

In some classrooms the power and authority is placed solely with the class teacher. These classrooms are characterised by the majority of the decisions relating to learning coming from the teacher, the teacher being seen as the 'holder' of information whose job is to impart it to the children and an extremely structured approach to the curriculum which 'rolls on' regardless. In an imaginative classroom often the teacher needs to readjust the power base, seeing the children as joint collaborators in their learning, influencing the direction it takes and the questions raised. The teacher works alongside the children as an active learner guiding and supporting them along the journey. To some this may sound too free with a lack of direction. This is the challenge. For the teacher to adjust the power base in the class they need to take a risk. They need to allow the needs and experiences of the children, sometimes unknown to the teacher, to influence the curriculum: too free and the class will lose direction, too structured and the curriculum will not be relevant to the needs of the children. Instead of focusing on 'delivering' a lesson or curriculum to a group of children the teacher will be using their pedagogic understanding to develop and support the learning taking place.

Let us now return to Alphen (2011) and identify some of the benefits of creating a curriculum which values and fosters imagination. Alphen (2011) notes the following benefits:

- Imaginative teaching engages the 'whole child' in the process of learning.
- Children are able to connect with their subject material in a way that is possible at their stage of development, that is, by means of the imagination.
- When teachers appeal to the imagination in their lessons, learners become engrossed in the subject matter and willingly participate in the learning process.

- Such teachers show a flexibility of mind that enables them to present a subject in a new and engaging way, a way that enables students to understand it better and also take pleasure from learning.

In an imaginative classroom therefore the teacher, other adults and the children will be learning together. Curiosity should be fostered though authentic situations where learners want to explore the issues. There may not be any set answers but instead children will be grappling with a world of possibilities, stretching their thinking, reasoning and evaluative skills. The ideas in this book show how teaching can be centred on problems, emotions and challenges to be explored.

Our challenge as educators however is to evaluate our own pedagogy, identify what our ideas and assumptions are based on and to possibly reassess our practice to ensure that our teaching recognises and values the imaginative experiences we can provide for our children. This will ensure a connection to the emotions which will give authenticity to the work we embark on and will serve to engage with children's hopes, fears and intentions.

TEACHING THROUGH DRAMA

The title of this book focuses on drama. As with imagination, the term drama can bring with it a range of stereotypes or preconceptions which need addressing. What comes into your head when the word 'drama' is mentioned? Maybe, seeing as you are reading this book, you already have a good idea of the concept of drama within the classroom, but for some it will conjure up images of rearranging furniture, finding open space or finding time for drama on 'special' occasions or 'after the work is done'. For others the word may fill them with dread conjuring up memories of being taught drama or attending drama workshops. Drama is an all-encompassing term for a range of conventions used within education and also outside education. The use of the term 'drama' within our context for this book needs to be defined more closely in order for us to understand the type of drama conventions and practices this book will focus on.

DEFINING DRAMA

We can think of drama in terms of a continuum ranging from formal drama on one side to informal drama on the other. Formal drama may be characterised as presenting in front of an audience with a script where a director has picked, possibly through auditions, the most suitable person for each role. The actors are told what to say, how to say it and when to say it. Theatre productions, school shows and assemblies often characterise formal drama. On the other end of the continuum we will find free play where children may be involved in self-generated role play. They may, for example, be in the playground recreating a scene from a story they have read or from a television programme. This type of drama is characterised often by spontaneity and the fact that there is no audience present. The drama we are focused upon within this book is what

Taylor and Warner (2006) term process drama, Booth (1994) calls story drama and Grainger and Cremin (2001) call classroom drama, which is located centrally on our drama continuum.

Within process drama children 'are involved in working imaginatively to improvise and sustain the different roles that they choose to adopt, offering ideas to develop and shape the unfolding drama and contributing to the problem-solving agenda' (Cremin & McDonald, 2013 p. 85). The problem-solving agenda is crucial in process drama as the participants need to feel something in order to invest in the drama and value the experience. In the section which contains examples of drama activities based around a range of texts there will always be a problem which needs solving. That could be for example the dilemma facing the Captain on the Rita Anne in the text *The Wretched Stone* who needs to decide how to save his boat and his crew from certain death, or Hosea in Michael Morpurgo's *Blodin the Beast* who needs to carry out the instructions of Shanga in order to save the people in his village from slavery. It is how we create the authenticity of the problem and the desire to solve the problem which is one of our roles within the classroom. It is also our willingness to move away from the plans and the direction of the lesson in order to 'seize the moment' (Cremin, Goouch, Blakemore, Goff, & McDonald, 2006) in response to the living drama as it unfolds.

THE BENEFITS OF PROCESS DRAMA

Process drama will connect to the emotions of the participants often through the tension which is experienced within the drama. This emotional engagement is experienced due to the nature of all the participants coming in and out of the drama experience. Earlier on we spoke about the power base within the classroom and how the imaginative teacher is able to adjust the power base to reflect the collaborative learning taking place. This will be evident in process drama by the teacher working alongside the children as teacher in role (TiR). The drama is not '*for*' the children '*given*' by the teacher but instead the teacher works from within the drama to mould, encourage, model and move the drama on. The drama teaching will build on the positive relationships which exist between the children and the teachers, resulting in trusting interactions (Wyse & Jones, 2008). By doing this the teacher will enable 'children to inhabit places and situations previously unknown to them' (McDonald, 2013 p. 71) in a safe environment where they are free to experiment with their own thoughts, perceptions and emotions. Therefore from within the drama the participants will be working imaginatively, taking risks, discovering the unknown and be involved in possibility thinking.

We defined imagination earlier as the ability to think of the possible rather than the actual and can now see how this is crucial to process drama where we encourage children to enter into possibility thinking. Possibility thinking, which is at the heart of creativity (Craft, 2000), involves finding ways to cope with problems, trying out possibilities and identifying questions for investigation. It is also characterised by the ability of the teacher to stand back, giving children the time to immerse themselves imaginatively within the problem-solving context. These characteristics are also employed as part of process drama within the classroom.

Drama therefore 'fosters children's creative engagement and enriches their imaginative development' (Cremin and McDonald, 2013 p. 83) and has the opportunity to enable children to experience a true purpose through the empowerment it gives them. The benefits of drama are manifold and have been acknowledged by many authors. Cremin, McDonald, Goff and Blakemore (2009 p. 1) summarise the benefits from a classroom position, stating that drama

- develops the imagination;
- creates affective and cognitive engagement;
- generates talk;
- enables a variety of voices to be heard;
- enriches writing opportunities;
- deepens understanding of texts;
- bridges the gap between genres;
- creates alternative perspectives;
- increases opportunities for storytelling;

In addition Wyse and Jones (2008) note that drama within the classroom can also help develop an awareness of oneself which may be difficult in other subjects. I would argue that if we are 'teaching through drama' as opposed to 'teaching drama' then the benefits will be encountered across the curriculum. Drama should not be seen as the 'tool' which is being brought out on a Friday when we go to the hall to explore the text we have been working through in terms of reading and writing, but instead should be the means by which we deepen our understanding of a text, a situation or an event as an ongoing basis 'seizing the moment' when most appropriate.

Drama and the imagination are therefore inextricably linked. Imagination is crucial for the drama to be able to connect with the participants in an authentic way presenting a problem-solving agenda which needs to be explored. The ideas in this book show how this can be achieved through carefully selected texts which form the basis of the drama work creating curiosity and intrigue.

REFERENCES

Alphen, P. (2011). Imagination as a transformative tool in primary school education. *Research on Steiner Education, 2*(2), 16–34.

Booth, D. (1994). *Story drama: reading, writing and role playing across the curriculum.* Markham: Pembroke.

Craft, A. (2000). *Creativity across the primary curriculum: framing and developing Practice.* London: Routledge.

Cremin, T., Goouch, K., Blakemore, L., Goff, E., & McDonald, R. (2006). Connecting drama and writing: seizing the moment to write. *Research in Drama Education, 11*(3), 273–91.

Cremin, T., & McDonald, R. (2013). Drama. In R. Jones, & D. Wyse (eds), *Creativity in the Primary Curriculum* (pp. 83–97). London: Routledge.

Cremin., T., McDonald, R., Goff, E., & Blakemore, L. (2009). *Jumpstart drama.* London: David Fulton.

Egan, K. (1992). *Imagination in teaching and learning: the middle school years.* Chicago: University of Chicago Press.

Egan, K. (2005) *An imaginative approach to teaching.* San Francisco: Jossey-Bass.

Grainger, T., & Cremin, M. (2001). *Resourcing classroom drama 5–8.* Sheffield: National Association for the Teaching of English.

Lefstein, A., & Snell, J. (2014). *Better than best practice: developing teaching and learning through dialogue.* London: Routledge.

McDonald, R. (2013). *The primary teacher's guide to speaking and listening.* London: Scholastic.

McKernan, J. (2008). *Curriculum and imagination.* London: Routledge.

Taylor, P., & Warner, C. D. (2006). *Structure and spontaneity: the process drama of Cecily O'Neil.* Stoke on Trent: Trentham.

Warnock, M. (1976). *Imagination.* Berkeley: University of California Press.

Wyse, D., & Jones, R. (2008). *Teaching English language and literacy.* London: Routledge.

3 Teaching with texts at the heart

THE POWER OF PICTUREBOOKS

Picturebooks are at the core of all of the ideas in this book. Each teaching sequence introduces a text to the children and encourages them to enter into a deeper understanding of the characters, context, situation and dilemmas through the use of interactive strategies including drama conventions. This approach is characterised by the teacher working alongside the children as joint collaborators in learning. Ideas are presented for use across the primary phase using texts chosen specifically for their ability to engage all learners. Although age guidelines are given, most ideas can, of course be adapted to be appropriate for other age groups. It is important that we use picturebooks with our older learners as they are rich resources which provide ample opportunity for exploration. I often used the wordless picturebook *The Arrival* by Shaun Tan with my class of 10- and 11-year-olds. Their preconceptions of a wordless picture book would often relate to memories of the type they were accustomed to in their early school years. They found it fascinating therefore to find themselves reading *The Arrival*, interpreting events, discussing points of view and searching for meaning. We concluded that the fact that it was wordless made it more complex than if it had text.

The complexity of picturebooks is of interest to us as many of the examples within this book use picturebooks as the stimulus. When reading picturebooks we are generating meaning by bringing our own experiences to the text, reading the pictures, reading the text and understanding the book as a whole. Indeed Serafini (2009) notes that 'the picture book is a unique experience, where meaning is generated simultaneously from written text, visual images and the overall design' (Serafini, 2009 p. 10). Through reading picturebooks the text and pictures 'take on a meaning that neither possesses without the other' (Nodelman, 1998 p. 223) meaning that we must explore both and resist the temptation to simply follow the text which often encourages us to turn the page. Indeed 'rushing through a picturebook may mean that we do not do ourselves or the text justice as the power of the text and illustrations are not given the chance to weave their magic' (McDonald, 2014 p. 156). Instead we should explore the pictures equally, noticing whether they complement the text, add to the text or seemingly work against the text.

You may see various spellings of 'picturebook' such as picture book, picture-book or picturebook (Booker, 2012). Here the joining of the words picture and book is deliberate. The union, which Wolfenbarger and Sipe (2007) examine, which exists between the illustrations and the text is important as we need both in order to make meaning although in postmodern picturebooks the illustrations and text sometimes seem to tell diverging stories.

THE SOPHISTICATION OF PICTUREBOOKS

There are a number of studies which help distinguish between different types of picturebook. Here I will highlight two studies. These are useful as we can use them to identify the characteristics of a picturebook we may intend to use and thereby consider its suitability for the class we are teaching.

The first study was undertaken by Lewis (2001) who identifies a series of levels. Through the understanding of these levels Lewis exemplifies how we can identify the sophistication of a picturebook. The table below outlines his system and gives examples of the type of picturebook it may include.

Level	Characteristics	Example texts
1	The words and pictures are aligned closely with the intention of supporting early readers with their comprehension.	Examples include some of the many texts produced as a result of the focus on systematic synthetic phonics and also texts published before the postmodern era. *The Very Hungry Caterpillar* (1971, Puffin) by Eric Carle
2	The pictures can be manipulated which may affect the interpretation of the text. The words may be presented in a number of ways impacting on how they are interpreted.	*Charlie and Lola* (2007, Orchard Books) by Lauren Child *The Wolves in the Walls* (2004, Bloomsbury) by Neil Gaiman, illustrated by Dave McKean *Lydia Greenfingers* (2016, Austin Macauley) by Joseph Hopkins
3	The words and the pictures may drift apart from one another.	*Rosie's Walk* (2001, Red Fox) by Pat Hutchins *Beneath the Surface* (2005, Hodder Headline Australia) by Gary Crew, illustrated by Steven Woolman
4	The unexpected happens and readers' expectations are challenged. Characters may step out of one story into another.	*The Three Pigs* (2012, Anderson Press) by David Wiesner *Knuffle Bunny* (2005, Walker Books) by Mo Willems *Good Night, Gorilla* (2012, Egmont) by Peggy Rathmann *Bad Day at Riverbend* (1996, Houghton Mifflin) by Chris Van Allsburg

Although these levels can be useful they are not an indication of age-related texts and are not hierarchical. Children may need exposure to texts at all levels in order to be able to develop their confidence and competence at reading picturebooks.

The second study focuses specifically on postmodern picturebooks. These are books where the illustrators and authors 'deliberately work against a linear story-telling pattern' (Wolfenbarger and Sipe, 2007 p. 275). Goldstone (2002) brilliantly highlights how the postmodern picturebook stays true to the definition of a picturebook but is able to play with the underlying organisation which creates 'new linguistic codes' (Goldstone, 2002 p. 362). These codes have been identified as being related to four specific characteristics related to postmodern picturebooks as shown in the table below.

Code	Description	Example texts
Nonlinearity	These books do not follow the traditional story grammar but instead the story parts may be jumbled, meaning the reader may go back as well as forward.	*Tales of the Dead* (2004, Dorling Kindersley) by Stewart Ross and Richard Bonson *Snowflake Bentley* (2009, Houghton Mifflin Harcourt) by Jacqueline Bentley *One Tiny Turtle* (2015, Walker Books) by Nicola Davies
Self-referential text	Self-referential texts refer to the way the book itself has been created. In these texts characters can sometimes step out of the book, with the reader encouraged to question the 'fictional reality of the story' (Booker, 2012 p. 2).	*The Story of a Little Mouse Trapped in a Book* (1981, Heinemann) by Monique Felix *Art and Max* (2015, Andersen Press) by David Wiesner *What's Wrong with this Book?* (2011, Corraini) by Richard McGuire
The sarcastic or mocking tone	These texts have a tone which playfully mocks reality and is centred on our preconceived expectations. As readers we question the characters and often the story itself. Fairy tales are often used in this way as they take the traditional and subvert the story and the characters in a myriad of ways.	*Cinderella's Rat* (1997, Houghton Mifflin) by Susan Meddaugh *Snow White in New York* (1989, OUP) by Fiona French *The True Story of the Three Little Pigs* (1991, Puffin) by Jon Scieszha.
Anti-authoritarian text	In these texts it is clear that the author is not making all the decisions and instead the reader is, at times, seen as a co-author of the narrative. Bringing personal knowledge the reader builds understanding together with the author.	*Come Away from the Water, Shirley* (1992, Red Fox) by John Burningham *Tuesday* (2012, Andersen Press) by David Wiesner *David Goes to School* (2001, Scholastic) by David Shannon

In the postmodern world in which we live with television, web spaces and the on-demand culture requiring the need for the consumer to make links between different aspects, follow more than one thread at once, disregard irrelevant information and make individual choices, it is not surprising that the picturebook also requires these skills from the reader. The important point is that we, as educators, need to recognise the changing culture of reading and acknowledge that reading changes and we (both adults and children) have to continue to learn to read (Meek, 1992).

We need to adjust our questioning to reflect the non-linear texts we are likely to use within the classroom in order to encourage children to make intertextual connections. Goldstone (1999) offers some pertinent advice in order to foster a greater understanding of these picturebooks, which is summarised below.

1   Focus on the interconnections of the multiple story lines by exploring whether the stories occur at the same time, whether the behaviour and characteristics of the characters are similar or different, what the mood of each story is and whether each story can stand alone.
2   Describe to the children how you read the text. You could model this out loud for them showing how you may need to reread, go backwards and forwards in the text. Voice the process and ask questions of yourself and of the text. Point out any changes in rhythm, mood or story structure.
3   Discuss the illustrations and talk about how they play a pivotal role in the story. Ask children to look at the style, colour and composition of the illustrations. Are there differences between the illustrations for the different storylines? Focus on how we read the illustrations and whether this is in fact harder than reading text.
4   Children could write their own non-linear text. You could model it on one of the texts mentioned in the box above or through the texts chosen alongside the themes in this book.

We therefore need to teach children how to read postmodern picturebooks. One way is through the activities in this book which encourage the children and the teacher to work together discovering and creating the narrative through playful interactions. Through engaging with the texts presented in this book children will experience the unexpected, find themselves as co-authors of the narrative and will feel the importance of recognising their own backgrounds and experiences.

PICTUREBOOKS AND THE TEACHING OF GRAMMAR

It seems that most books for teachers published in the last 3 years include a section on grammar. In this book it is deliberately brief. This does not reflect the place grammar has within teaching creativity through drama. On the contrary, teaching in this way will enable children to reflect on their language choices and refine them. It is brief because the teaching of grammar should be seen as integral within the context of the drama rather than as a separate entity or add on.

Since the introduction of the new national curriculum (2013) and the subsequent changes to assessment at Key Stage One and Key Stage Two there has been a renewed interest and focus on the teaching of grammar. This is an important, necessary and potentially playful element of our teaching which, when embedded as part of the ongoing work we are doing, can enrich children's ability to manipulate language. However once again we need to question our pedagogy. How are we teaching grammar in our classroom and what is the research evidence for the pedagogy we choose? As Alexander (2010) notes, we need a pedagogy of repertoire and principle rather than recipe and prescription with teaching fully rather than selectively informed by research.

THE IMPORTANCE OF TEACHING GRAMMAR

Teaching grammar is really teaching about the use of language. For any reader or writer to be reflective and critical then knowledge of language and how it is organised to make meaning is essential.

Reedy and Bearne (2013) note that grammar is the study of how we make sense in speaking and writing so that we can understand people who speak the same language as we do. They continue to say that understanding grammar is more than a matter of learning just to name parts of speech; it's a matter of understanding how language works so that we can write or say exactly what we want to say as effectively as possible.

It is important to keep in mind the purpose of teaching grammar. As Waugh, Warner and Waugh (2013) note teaching grammar is not simply about being confident in correcting mistakes in children's work or to pass on 'tricks and techniques to be replicated in a mechanical way' (p. 7). This does not lead to good writing or developing good writers. Cremin and Myhill (2011) note that some formulaic strategies used ignore the influence of reading on writing.

Research indicates that the most effective practice is one where children 'make connections between grammar and writing, or between grammar and meaning' (Myhill, Lines, & Watson, 2011 p. 3).

It is the aim of this book that teachers using it will feel compelled to look at the research evidence relating to the teaching of grammar and look for opportunities in the work they are already doing to teach grammar in context. It is hoped that a reader of this book will conclude that 'the teaching of grammar goes far beyond the ability to succeed in end of key stage tests' and that it is 'about being able to choose and use language well for a wide range of purposes and audience, and being able to harness the power that writing offers' (Waugh, Warner, & Waugh, 2013 p. 9).

Readers will understand the importance of making the connection between grammatical content and writing when teaching guided reading, modelled writing, shared writing and guided writing so that children see how the language choices they make impact on the reader/listener. Grammar therefore is not separate from imaginative engagement through drama but integral to it. Children, when placed at the heart of the drama, will find themselves stretching for the language needed to express their opinions, points of view and desires. Through modelling and scaffolding within an authentic situation children will be able to make language choices which could strengthen the drama experienced.

REFERENCES

Alexander, R. (2010). Speaking but not listening? Accountable talk in an unaccountable context. *Literacy, 44*(3), 103–11.

Booker, K. (2012) Using picturebooks to empower and inspire readers and writers in the upper primary classroom. *Literacy Learning: The Middle Years, 20*(2), 1–14.

Cremin, T., & Myhill, D. (2011). *Writing voices: creating communities of writers.* London: Routledge.

Goldstone, B. (1999). Travelling in new directions: teaching non-linear picture books. *The Dragon Lode, 18*(1), 26–9.

Goldstone, B. (2002). Whaz up with our books? Changing picture book codes and teaching implications. *The Reading Teacher, 55*, 362–9.

Lewis, D. (2001). *Reading contemporary picturebooks: picturing text.* London: Routledge.

McDonald, R. (2014). Picture books. In V. Bower (ed.), *Developing early literacy 0 to 8: from theory to practice* (pp. 153–68). London: Sage.

Meek, M. (1992). Children reading – now. In M. Styles, E. Bearne, & V. Watson (eds), *After Alice: exploring children's literature* (pp. 172–87). London: Cassell.

Myhill, D., Lines, E., & Watson, A. (2011). Making meaning with grammar: a repertoire of possibilities. *Metaphor, 2*, 1–10.

Nodelman, P. (1998). *Words about pictures: the narrative art of children's picture books.* Athens: University of Georgia Press.

Reedy, D., & Bearne, E. (2013). *Teaching grammar effectively in primary schools.* London: United Kingdom Literacy Association.

Serafini, F. (2009). Understanding visual images in picturebooks. In J. Evans (ed.), *Talking beyond the page* (pp. 10–25). London: Routledge.

Waugh, D., Warner, C., & Waugh, R. (2013). *Teaching grammar, punctuation and spelling in primary schools.* London: Sage.

Wolfenbarger, C., & Sipe, L. (2007). A unique visual and literary art form: recent research on picturebooks. *Review of Research: Language Arts, 84*(3), 273–80.

4 Drama conventions
Creative strategies to use in the classroom

A range of drama conventions exist, which can be blended in classroom drama. Individually each creates different demands and prompts particular kinds of thinking and interaction appropriate at certain moments in the drama. They are not, however, rigid structures and can be adapted to suit the dramatic exploration and used flexibly during the session. It is hoped that you will use this chapter as a point of reference as you read the creative ideas related to texts.

The descriptions below have been adapted, with permission, from work first published by Grainger (now Cremin) in 1992.

STORYTELL

Throughout the ideas presented in this book, you will come across points where you are asked to 'storytell' or narrate parts of a story. This is an important strategy where the teacher becomes the storyteller. It enables you to go beyond the printed text and take the children to places they may not have considered. In essence you are embellishing parts of the text, reading between the lines and exploring the possibilities. Through storytelling you will be building tension, changing the pace and including children's ideas as part of the narration. The joy of this convention is that there will not be any perceived 'right' answers as you will be entering into the unknown with the children.

FREEZE FRAME

This convention is also known as creating tableaux, still images or statue making. Individually, in small groups or as a whole class, the children use their bodies to create an image of an event, an idea, a theme or a moment in time. This still silent picture, freezes the action, as do newspaper pictures, but it can also portray a visual memory, or a wish, or show an image from a dream, as well as represent more abstract themes such as anger, jealousy or the truth. Freeze frames can also be brought to life, and can be subtitled with an appropriate caption, written or spoken, or have noises and sound effects added to them. In addition the words or inner thoughts of members of the tableau can be voiced when the teacher touches children on the shoulder. Freeze frames offer a useful way of capturing and conveying meaning, since groups can convey much more than they would be able to through words alone.

GROUP SCULPTURE

Similar to a freeze-frame the group will make a sculpture with their bodies to depict a theme, concept or issue arising from the story. Often taking place at the end of a story when time has been given to contemplate the meaning, children, working in small groups, will represent what the story meant to them. For example in the wordless picturebook *Why* by Nikolai Popov, children may use group sculpture to convey the themes of destruction, helplessness, consequences or jealously.

HOT SEATING

In this convention, the teacher and/or the children assume the role of one or more individuals from the drama and are questioned by the remainder of the class. The class need to be forewarned and primed to think of questions. They can ask the questions either as themselves, so their point of view is outside the drama, or they can adopt a role within the drama and ask questions from this perspective. If the class is in role, this helps to focus the kind of questions asked and may prompt the need for notes to be taken. This is a useful probing technique which seeks to develop knowledge of the characters' motives, attitudes and behaviour. It encourages increased reflective awareness of the complex nature of human behaviour.

IMPROVISATION: SMALL GROUP

Improvisation can be prepared beforehand or spontaneously developed. In small groups children, discuss, plan and then create a piece of prepared improvisation. This kind of improvisation is relatively secure, because through their discussion they create a kind of script or structure to follow.

IMPROVISATION: WHOLE CLASS

The whole class, including the teacher, engage in improvisation together. Again such improvisation can be planned or spontaneous. It can be 'formal' as in a whole-class meeting, for example, a court scene, or more informal, a class improvisation of a market scene, or the railway station, shortly before a major incident occurs. Whole-class role play reduces the pressure of being watched since everyone is corporately engaged and lives in the moment responding to each other naturally in the imaginary context.

TEACHER IN ROLE

This is the most powerful convention the teacher has at their disposal. It involves the teacher engaging fully in the drama by taking various roles. This technique is a tool through which the teacher can support, extend and challenge the children's thinking from inside the drama. The teacher in role can influence events from within the developing situation. Every role has its own social status which gives access to an influence commensurate with its position. High-status roles have a controlling and deciding nature, while lower-status roles are not so openly powerful, but can still be influential.

THOUGHT TRACKING

In this convention, the private thoughts of individuals are shared publicly. This can be organised in different ways; the teacher can touch individuals on the shoulder during a freeze-frame, or halt an improvisation, and ask them to voice their thoughts. Or the whole class can take on the persona of one individual and simultaneously speak out loud their thoughts and fears in a particular situation. Alternatively, the teacher, or a child, in role, can give witness to the class and speak personally about recent events from a 'special' chair, or members of the class can take turns in moving forward to stand behind the chair and express their thoughts about the character. This convention is useful to slow down the action and can prompt both deeper understanding of individual characters and sensitive responses to what has happened.

FORUM THEATRE

This is an improvisation performed by a few members of the class in the forum of the classroom, which then is discussed, revisited and developed. In its simplest form, an important situation is improvised and watched by the class, and the words and actions of those involved are commented upon, (with the helpful mediation of the teacher) and then the same situation is reworked taking into account what has been said. A development of this technique is to offer the children, actors or observers, the chance to stop the action, suggest changes and justify their alternative ideas. This convention allows the drama to be revisited, making use of many of their ideas. It is valuable for examining difficult situations more closely and working out how they might best be tackled.

ROLE ON THE WALL

In this convention, an outline is drawn around an important character as they lie upon a large piece of paper, and then information and feelings about the character are written into the shape by each child. This can be added to throughout the drama. It can also be enriched by being written from different perspectives, for example, the space outside the outline can contain comments about the character as they are seen from an observer's viewpoint and the interior space can contain the character's own thoughts and point of view. This is a valuable convention for building a deep understanding of a chosen role.

DECISION ALLEY

This convention refers to any situation in which there are different choices of action, conflicting interests or dilemmas. It is useful to examine the pros and cons of a decision. Two lines of children face each other, approximately two paces apart and reasonably spaced out. One child in role walks slowly down the alley between them. As the character progresses down the alley, their thoughts or the sets of views for and against a course of action, which the role faces, are voiced out loud by the rest of the class. The character can then be hot seated at the end of the alley, to establish their final decision and to understand why they have made this choice.

WRITING IN ROLE

A variety of kinds of writing can emerge from the lived experience of the drama and can be written in role, for example, letters, diaries, messages, pamphlets, notes, even graffiti. For example, in a drama about opening a local tourist shop, a multitude of forms of writing may be involved, including adverts for jobs, fliers about the shop, interior designs, letters of information to the press, display resumes, as well as diaries of the workers, newspaper reports, scripts for a radio item, and so on. Children often write with considerable urgency in drama since they have a purpose and a clearly imagined audience for their writing.

DRAWING

This involves the children individually or in small groups drawing a significant object in the drama. For example, a detailed drawing of some particular flora and fauna found during the migration west of the American pioneers can help children invent possibilities and sow seeds for future action. In this way the drawing enhances the drama and creates new meanings.

OVERHEARD CONVERSATIONS

In small groups, conversations between characters are improvised, and then a few are 'overheard' by the class, to add tension and information, and to enable a range of viewpoints to be established. The group can also recreate key conversations from the past that shed light upon the present situation. The teacher as storyteller may later integrate these perspectives into the drama.

RITUAL OR CEREMONY

In ritual, the teacher and the class together work out ways of marking significant events in the narrative and create some form of ceremony which is part of the drama. Such rituals often slow the drama down and provoke a deepening sense of significance, as well as reflection. For example, the children as villagers might create a chant or simple dance to thank their gods for their beneficence, or in another drama, different villagers might write prayers and make artefacts to leave at the burial site of their shaman. Ritual is often used to conclude work or to intensify the tenor of the drama.

MANTLE OF THE EXPERT

This convention involves children being given or adopting roles, which necessarily include the expertise, authority, knowledge and skill of specialists. Their expertise is explicitly used in the drama. This knowledge may be recently acquired from classroom research, or it might be their own personal expertise, but the status it gives the children, allows them to significantly influence the drama. The teacher must honour the expertise and may therefore take on a role of relative ignorance in the drama, or assume a more equal role alongside them.

CREATING A SOUNDSCAPE

This convention involves using body percussion or the voice to create an atmosphere at significant points within a story. The soundscape could accompany a freeze-frame, the narration of the story or be part of a role play. Soundscapes encourage children to experiment with body percussion in order to convey a mood. For example in *The Watertower* by Gary Crew one of the characters sits alone in the tower while the water eddies and swirls beneath him. This is a superb opportunity to create a mysterious atmosphere.

None of these conventions are fixed and unchangeable, you'll find you can change them to suit your purposes, adapting them to the needs of the drama, and if you create new ones for yourself so much the better.

PART 2

Creative ideas with texts

5 Creative ideas with texts
Suspense

If we think about books we have read or films we have seen it is often the feeling of suspense which keeps us watching or turning the page. We have a desire to solve the problem or resolve the situation. Within this genre there is a gap between what we know and what we want to know. This gap is purposefully left by the author and is a perfect space for our imaginations to take shape and explore a world of possibilities. Often the author will simply drop a piece of information into the gap which may confirm, deny or complicate our initial thoughts. Suspense works well to connect a range of our emotions to the text, sometimes causing us to be disturbed but, within the safe and playful environment of the classroom, we are able to explore our emotions and solve the problem presented to us.

THE MINPINS (2008, PUFFIN) BY ROALD DAHL, ILLUSTRATED BY PATRICK BENSON

- **Possible writing opportunity:** Descriptive writing, adverts, describing sculptures
- **Interactive strategies**: Role play, decision alley, freeze-frame, teacher in role (TiR), improvisation, drawing
- **Age range**: 5–9

Introduction

Roald Dahl is one of the country's best-known authors. In 2012 Roald Dahl was voted primary school teachers' favourite author. It is important to introduce children to a range of familiar authors as well as expanding children's knowledge of unfamiliar authors.

The Minpins is a fascinating and enchanting picturebook in which we follow the adventures of Billy, a young boy who, at the start of the text, is bored. We are told that all the things he wants to do are exciting and all the things he is allowed to do are boring – a theme which may well resonate with some of our children! Billy is in the predicament of having been told that he must not venture out of the back gate and enter the forest. His mother has even made up a rhyme to persuade him not to go:

'Beware, beware the forest of sin,
None come out but many go in.'

Inevitably Billy does creep out of the house, go through the gate and enter the forest. This is where the adventures begin for Billy as he comes face to face with the very creature his mother has warned him about! Roald Dahl captures the sense of despair, regret and loneliness as Billy wishes he had heeded his mother's advice. However as Billy scrambles up a tree to safety, Billy enters the unfamiliar world of the Minpins. He soon hatches a plan to save both himself and his new friends and successfully succeeds in overcoming the Gruncher.

Teaching objectives

- Understand and take pleasure in the difference between pretence and reality.
- Identify with characters and actions through role playing.
- Use a range of dramatic forms to express ideas and feelings.
- Gain confidence in their own abilities, particularly to communicate verbally and non-verbally.
- Contribute ideas through using the imagination.

Problems, emotions or challenges to be explored

- The first issue involves the voices in Billy's head. When Billy is bored he needs to wrestle with his conscious and consider whether to go against his mother's advice.
- The second issue is concerned with the realisation that what his mother had told him, all the stories and warnings about the creature in the forest were true. What other 'perceived myths' which adults say are also true?
- The third issue is about keeping secrets. At the end of the story we are told that Billy continues to meet with the Minpins but has never and will never ever tell a soul about their existence.

The session

The ideas presented are intended to be adapted and shaped by you for use in your class. They are not intended as a formula to follow or as a lesson plan. You may feel that you would like, for example, to take one idea and expand on it depending on the interests of your class or you may want to sequence a few of the ideas together. The text should help inspire teaching with a purpose which creates passion and empowers the class. This will depend, not only on the interests of your class, but also on your characteristics as a teacher. Some ideas will resonate more strongly with you than others. I hope the ideas you do use and embellish will mean that your class encounters imaginative teaching with purpose and passion for empowerment.

Connecting with the author and illustrator

Display a range of books by Roald Dahl. Discuss with the class which ones they have read and take feedback. Start to draw out the characteristics of Dahl's writing. Discuss the fact that when we start a new book by Roald Dahl we have certain expectations regarding the characters, language and plot. Explore the effect of this on the reader.

Explain that one of the powerful aspects of this book is the extraordinary pictures. Spend time looking at the work of Patrick Benson who in 1984 won the Mother Goose Award for the most promising newcomer in children's book illustrations. Children may be familiar with the book *Owl Babies* by Martin Waddell which Patrick also illustrated. In addition in 1990 Patrick authored and illustrated the text *Little Penguin*.

Making connections to the text

Display the front and back cover of the text *The Minpins*. Spend time exploring the front cover. Children will notice the boy in the clearing of the forest and in time will also notice the little people on the branches. Consider the situation and ask the children what the little people may be thinking. Children will draw on their own understanding of the natural environment and issues of power relations with the animal world. Explore a range of possibilities with the children by exploring questions such as:

- Would the little people be concerned about the boy?
- What leads you to think this?
- Do you think they often see people in the forest?
- What is it about the way the little people are depicted which leads you to think this?
- Do you think that the boy has noticed the little people?
- What would be his reaction if he saw them?
- What would you do?

Tell the children that the story is about a boy who is referred to in the text as 'Little Billy'. Pose the thought which will encourage children to consider why Roald Dahl specifically uses the word 'little' rather than simply 'Billy'. Explain that the story is about the boy being tempted to do something his mother has told him not to do. Share a story from your own childhood of a situation when you really wanted to do something or explore somewhere but had been warned against it by your parents. Give time for children to share their own stories in small groups.

Read the first page making connections to the stories the children shared about their own lives. The picture shows Billy gazing out of the window. The garden gate is in the centre of the picture signifying its importance. Consider what might be going through Billy's mind as he sits gazing out to the garden. You might want to use large thought bubbles and invite children in pairs or groups to write their idea of what Billy would be thinking. It may be appropriate to stick the thought bubbles on the classroom window next to an empty chair which would depict the scene from the text. Alternatively you may want to set up the scene in the classroom and invite a child to sit gazing out of the window.

Other children are then invited to come up, touch the chair and speak, out loud, what Billy may be thinking at this time. These thoughts will be added to later in the lesson.

Read the second page up to the line '"I'm being good, Mummy", Little Billy called back'.' Aim to build up a description of the forest according to Billy's mother. Read the page stopping to note the description. You could collect some of the description on a flipchart. Ask the children to consider whether Billy would believe his mother. Make the connection to the children's own lives by discussing any instances when they have been told 'stories' to prevent them from doing something.

Encountering temptation

Towards the end of the second page of text we encounter Billy's first predicament. He starts to hear a voice in his head which Roald Dahl describes as 'the devil'. When working in the classroom I refer to this as Billy's conflicting conscience. This is a superb point to explore Billy's stream of thoughts resulting from the temptation to ignore the warnings from his mother and go and explore the forest. In small groups encourage children to think about the reasons why he may want to go and also reasons why he should stay at home. Children may want to refer to the work earlier in the lesson where his initial thoughts about boredom were explored and also the description from his mother about the dangers of the forest. Aim to listen in to the group discussions adding your own views to the conversations to encourage children to consider the consequences of their initial suggestions and also to support them in extending their ideas.

Use the drama convention of 'decision alley' which is also sometimes known as the 'thought tunnel' or 'conscience corridor'. The aim is to give children the opportunity to voice Billy's thoughts. Invite children to form two lines facing each other in the classroom. Choose one child to take on the role of Billy. Billy will slowly walk down the corridor listening to the conflict in his own mind voiced by the children forming the lines. Once Billy has walked the corridor give him time to consider what he has heard and then decide on his course of action. It is important that you honour the decision Billy makes and so if, on balance, he decides to go home then you will need to weave this decision into the story. You could for example, before reading page 8, narrate 'days passed and the voices in Billy's head got louder and louder. The voices were so persuasive . . .'

Read page 8 pausing to note how the voices use persuasive techniques to convince Billy of the benefits of entering the forest. Half way down this page Roald Dahl expertly compares Billy's outward actions to his inward feelings. Spend some time here looking at the language used. The page ends with a delicious sentence which, together with the picture on the adjacent page, sends a message of foreboding to the reader. Dahl writes 'it was like being among the dead in an enormous empty green cathedral'. This sentence is one which could be captured and displayed in order for us to refer to it later.

This is a suitable point to introduce a freeze-frame to the class. There is great symbolism of the giant trees surrounding Billy who looks so small, helpless and weak. Invite the children, in small groups, to create this scene. Support them with ways in which to show the contrast between Billy and the space he is in. Although trees will be represented in the freeze-frames you should encourage children to consider what the trees symbolise and therefore different ways they could represent this. There is a difference in size, in power, in knowledge, in safety and in wisdom. Encourage the children to make the freeze-frames to reflect this. Explain that once you count down 'five, four, three, two, one, freeze' each group should be in their freeze-frame and ready to share a caption which sums up the significance of their depiction.

Feeling alone in the forest

Explain that you want to hear what Billy is thinking at this point in the story. Give children time in their groups to discuss the thoughts, feelings, excitement, anticipation and trepidation that Billy may be experiencing. Encourage the children to create a sentence or two within the group which will convey this. Remind the children that they can use any of Billy's senses within their description. The time to discuss, talk, share, refine and craft their description is important. When the children are ready explain that you will count down again and groups should form their freeze-frames. You will then visit each group and Billy will voice their group's description. This works well if you can also narrate the story at this point. This forms synergy between the groups and the descriptions heard.

On page 11 the suspense is built as we realise that there is something in the forest and that his mother may have been right after all. The page ends with a wonderful sentence which just impels you to turn the page. Dahl writes '. . . and now, in the distance, he saw a sight that froze his blood and made icicles in his veins'. Wow! What a glorious sentence. This is a sentence I would capture and display for the children in order for them to use it in their own writing. Of course at this point children will want you to turn the page. Anticipation will have been built and the description of what Billy has heard and seen in the forest will leave pictures in the children's minds. Instead of turning the page invite the children to create their own representation of the Spittler. Hand out paper for the children to draw their idea of what the Spittler could look like. Encourage the children to talk and share their ideas on their tables. This could be extended and children could be provided with a range of materials in order to then construct their Spittler. Once the models have been made children could write descriptions of them for display.

The illustrations by Patrick Benson are truly brilliant and I would certainly spend time looking at them with the children. On the double-page spread which shows the fire bellowing down at Billy, encourage the children to look closely and see the clues about the Spittler which are within the picture.

Meeting the Minpins

Read on to page 17 where we are introduced to the Minpins. Read the page to the children noting the amount of detail Roald Dahl includes. Show them the page with the drawing removed. Explain that we are going to be Patrick Benson and are going to create the drawing which would accompany the description. Read the page again to the children noting the description and discussing which aspects could be represented through their drawings. Then give the children the text from the page in order to support their drawing. Once complete you could use a checklist of the description for children to mark their work. Then reveal the actual illustration and discuss which aspects Patrick Benson has included and which he has left out.

Billy is now in the world of the Minpins with so much to explore. However there would possibly be understandable caution from the Minpins' perspective. Read to the point on page 18 where Dahl writes 'The faces were silent, unmoving, almost ghost-like'. Move away from the printed text here and narrate that the Minpins had never seen anything like this before. They had heard of these creatures called humans but had never actually encountered one. Were they friendly? Would he harm them? What are his motives? The Minpins were unsure what to do. Suddenly as if through telepathy all the shutters closed tightly shut at exactly the same time. Billy could hear the frantic voices inside indicating fear, caution but also a sense of intrigue.

Making decisions

Continue to narrate the story, telling the children that the head Minpin decided that the only thing to do was to call his advisors together to discuss this unfolding situation. I would suggest that you adopt a TiR stance and become the head Minpin. Call for certain children to join you at your meeting table. The advisors may have specific roles, for example an advisor of the lower branches, an advisor for the higher branches, an advisor for the collection of food, an advisor for the protection and safety of the Minpins . . . You may have specific children in mind or you may want to offer it as an open opportunity by saying something like 'Now the advisor of the lower branches – where are you? I can't see you so you will need to put your hand up'.

Once you have your advisors around your table and each advisor has a specific responsibility you will need to lead the meeting, encouraging, through your questioning, children to consider the benefits and negative aspects of allowing Billy into your world. The other children in the class should represent the Minpin community and so at certain points in the meeting you should refer to them for their thoughts on what they have heard and any questions they might have.

At the end of the meeting, thank your advisors and explain that you will consider all of the options and will announce your decision to the whole Minpin community. Send your advisors back into the main class and then, still in role, explain that your decision is to support and help Billy to defeat the beast which has tormented your own community for so many years.

You can now return to the printed text, rejoining the story at the point where we left it where Dahl writes '*Now the tiny old man in the window . . .*'.

Concluding the drama

On pages 19–22 Billy is introduced to the houses within the branches where the Minpins live. There are many great opportunities for exploring imaginative possibilities at this point in the text. For example while Billy is peering through the window you could ask children to go into role as a Minpin and take Billy on a guided tour of the house, describing what Billy is able to see but also describing the areas of the house Billy is unable to see. Alternatively Billy may see the Minpin Estate Agent where houses are advertised for sale. Children could create a house advert for one of the Minpin houses.

The story continues with Billy and the Minpins working out a plan to rid the forest of the Gruncher. This section could be read in one sitting with the children or enjoyed over several readings.

It is once the Gruncher has been defeated that we encounter an interesting dilemma. The dilemma concerns the issue of keeping secrets. You could discuss with the class whether secrets should always be kept. Was Billy right to keep the secret of the Minpins? What would be the consequence if he told people his secret?

Make this your own

There are many opportunities to extend the work. You may want to explore the issue of secrets in more detail and take the story on further, imagining that Billy just could not keep such a secret to himself and told one of his friends who he took to see the Minpins.

This could build until eventually lots of people know about them. Explore what the result would be. Maybe some would try to capture the Minpins as pets or maybe they would be protected and humans and Minpins could live in harmony. You could look at real-life instances of humans finding a new species and what the results were.

*

THE WATERTOWER (1999, CROCODILE BOOKS USA) BY GARY CREW, ILLUSTRATED BY STEVEN WOOLMAN

- **Possible writing opportunities**: Descriptive writing, diary entry
- **Interactive strategies**: Role play, freeze-frame, soundscape, improvisation
- **Age range**: 9–11

Introduction

Set in the Australian outback we meet two boys Spike and Bubba who want to go up to the watertower for a swim. The watertower has stood on Shooters Hill for as many years as anyone can remember and casts its shadow over the area. The boys make their way up to the watertower despite being warned of the dangers by Spike's mother. Once there Spike goes straight in for a swim leaving a more hesitant Bubba sitting on the bottom rung of the ladder. On discovering that Bubba's clothes have disappeared Spike volunteers to run back home leaving Bubba at the watertower. However on his return something has changed. After emerging from the watertower Bubba has the same fixed expression which the other townsfolk have and, if you look carefully, you will see the mark of the watertower on the back of his hand. One of the hallmarks of some Gary Crew texts is the sense of mystery, questioning and uncertainty which leaves the reader searching for meaning long after the pages of the book have been closed.

Teaching objectives

- Develop willingness to accept and respect the ideas of others and to build on them.
- Identify with characters and actions through role playing.
- Explore the differences between right and wrong in simple moral dilemmas posed through drama.
- Use a range of dramatic forms to express ideas and feelings.
- Learn to respect and, where necessary, depend upon others.
- Contribute ideas through using the imagination.

Problems, emotions or challenges to be explored

- The first issue encountered concerns the dilemma of following the advice given by parents if the advice is not in line with what we actually want to do.
- The second problem is about going into dangerous situations against the advice of others who may know better.
- The third issue deals with fear and isolation. At one point in the text a character is isolated, in an unknown environment and is unsure who or what is within the surroundings.

The session

The ideas presented are intended to be adapted and shaped by you for use in your class. They are not intended as a formula to follow or as a lesson plan. You may feel that you would like, for example, to take one idea and expand on it depending on the interests of your class or you may want to sequence a few of the ideas together. The text should help inspire teaching with a purpose which creates passion and empowers the class. This will depend, not only on the interests of your class, but also on your characteristics as a teacher. Some ideas will resonate more strongly with you than others. I hope the ideas you do use and embellish will mean that your class encounters imaginative teaching with purpose and passion for empowerment.

Introducing the text

Display the front cover of the text and ask the children to make predictions about the story. In the conversation note the following features:

- *The author*: What other stories do we know? Is he a new author to us? What do we expect from his writing?

- *The title and illustrator*: Note the fact the title appears lengthways down the side of the front cover and the name of the illustrator is upside down. Show the children how you need to re-orientate the book in order to view these in the traditional manner. As you turn the book ask the children what clues this might give to the layout inside the book.

- *Colour*: Ask the children to describe the colours on the front cover. What do they associate these colours with? What genre might the book be? Note the radiating nature of the green light and the concentric rings emanating from the tower.

- *Illustrations*: Children may not know what a watertower is so you may need to explain some of the background. Some knowledge about the history and workings of a watertower could add an extra dimension when exploring the text. Children, for example, will understand the need for a watertower to be elevated in order to pressurize the water. This may influence their thoughts when, later in the text, the two boys enter the tower.

First encounters

Open the title page where you will notice you need to turn the book sideways in order to read the opening paragraph. Before reading the paragraph note the layout of the double page and how the story (*The Watertower* itself) has encroached into this part of the book. You may want to compare this title page with title pages from other books the children know. This will enable them to identify the similarities and differences.

Read the paragraph on the title page. Before reading it for a second time tell the children that you will be asking them what they know, think and wonder about the text at this point. After the second reading hand out different colour sticky notes. On one colour children will be invited to note down what they know about the watertower, on another colour what they think and on the third colour what they wonder or questions they might have. You may want to display large paper around the classroom where children could stick their notes. This is an interesting exercise as you will see, at a glance, where most sticky notes are placed. From my experience children often have more notes with questions than any other category. You could discuss this with the children and look at how the author Gary Crew manages to create so many questions in the reader's mind. The sticky notes could be kept and, as a class, you could see how many get answered through the course of the reading.

The illustrations give clues to the mysterious nature of the watertower and its influence over the town. You may want to use colour photocopies of the pictures at pertinent points throughout the text for children to explore. One idea would be to give the children, in groups, a range of pictures from the text. These could be given one at a time or all at once for the children to explore. Encourage them to ask questions, make predictions and hypothesise about the story.

Venturing up to the watertower

Read the first page which tells us that on a summer afternoon Spike and Bubba met for a swim. The text tells us that Spike's mother had told him it is dangerous up there. Recreate the scene in Spike's house when he asks his mother if he could go up to the watertower. In pairs one child will take the role of Spike and the other child will take the role of his mother. Count down from five to one. When you get to one Spike should pose the thought of going to the watertower to his mother. Allow the role play to run for a couple of minutes then stop the class and ask any children who were in role as Spike whether they heard a good reason why they should not go to the watertower. Collect these together on the flipchart and, referring back to the writing style of Gary Crew, look at which ones create an air of mystery and suspense. In order to give the children an opportunity to refine their ideas organise groups of four where there will be two children taking the role of Spike and two children taking the role of Spike's mother. Explain that in this role play the mother's task is to discourage Spike from going to the watertower without letting him know the true reason. Share the responses and add any to the flipchart which create a sense of suspense.

Continue to read to the point where we are told that a security fence used to keep trespassers out but now it lies flattened on the ground. Ask the children, in groups of four or five, to think about what may have caused the security fence to come down. You could weave this into the narrative by storytelling that rumours were rife around the town about the night the fence came down. Some townsfolk tell of hearing and seeing strange figures up at the water-tower that night, others say it was something trying to escape whereas some simply say it was the water board who took the fence down. Tell the children that one member of the town says that they have the only photograph of that night, at the moment the fence came down but has never shown it to anyone!

In their groups, children should form a freeze-frame of the image they believe is captured in the photograph. Give the children a short amount of time to discuss their ideas and to organise what their freeze-frame will look like. Introduce the idea of their freeze-frame having a caption. If the photograph is kept in an envelope what did the photographer write on the envelope to capture the essence of the photograph? Once groups have had an opportunity to think about their caption count down from five to zero. When you reach zero the groups should freeze. At this point, with all groups in their freeze-frames, storytell the rumours which went around the town about the night the fence came down. Go to each group in turn as you storytell and ask them to insert their caption into your narrative.

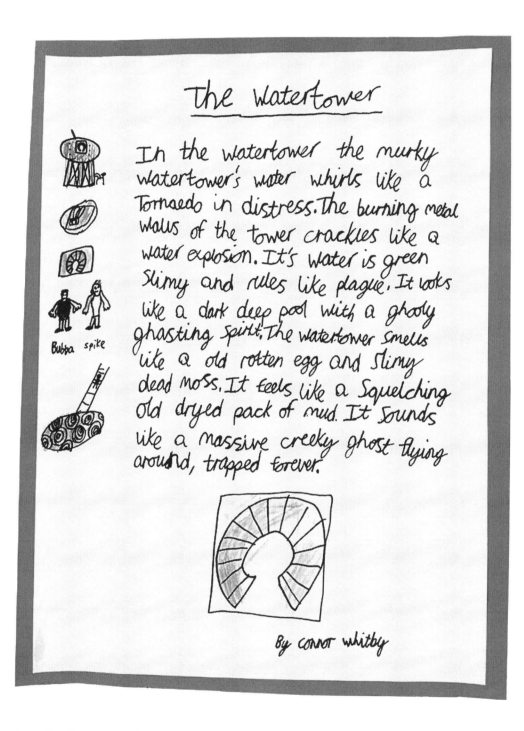

The Watertower

In the watertower the murky watertower's water whirls like a Tornaedo in distress. The burning metal walls of the tower crackles like a water explosion. It's water is green slimy and rules like plague. It looks like a dark deep pool with a ghooly ghasting spirit. The watertower smells like a old rotten egg and slimy dead moss. It feels like a squelching old dryed pack of mud. It sounds like a massive creeky ghost flying around, trapped forever.

Bubba   spike

By connor whitby

Figure 5.1 Description of the watertower

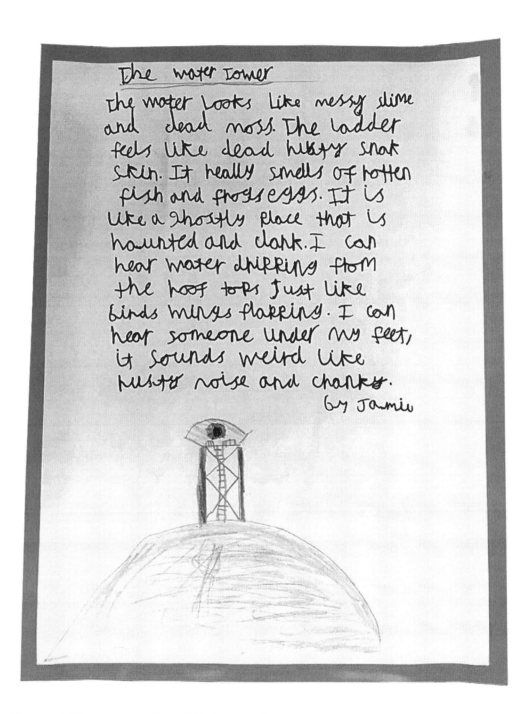

Figure 5.2 The watertower from Bubba's perspective

Creating the sounds of the watertower

Return to the text and continue reading to the point where Spike has gone into the watertower and Bubba is sat on the bottom rung. Discuss with the children the noises which Bubba might hear as he sits on the ladder. Construct a list of possibilities with the children. They may for example think of:

- creaking from the metal
- splashing of water
- dripping
- wind whistling through the tower
- echoes of Spike's wailing
- the beat of Bubbas heart.

Explain that, as a class, you are going to build a soundscape of the noises in the tower. Assign each group a noise to 'perform'. Give them some time to decide how they want theirs to sound which would complement the suspense genre. Allow groups to share their sounds with the rest of the class before putting them all together. It is useful if you indicate the volume by using your hand showing that five figures showing is the maximum volume and a clenched fist is silent. Practice the soundscape with the children and explain that later in the text they will need to be ready to use it as you read.

Continue reading and discussing the events surrounding the disappearance of Bubba's clothes. It is interesting that we are told on the first page that Bubba's mother could not have cared where he went but she would be angry about the lost clothes. Children may want to explore reasons for this. You could also explore why it was that only Bubba's clothes had disappeared? Was this coincidence or was someone or something aiming to separate the boys?

The page where Bubba climbs back down into the tank lends itself superbly to the use of the pre-rehearsed soundscape. As you are reading the page hold up your hand to indicate the start of the soundscape. Display one digit in order for the noises to start quietly, raising to a crescendo and then falling silent just before you read the words 'But he was frightened, very frightened'. You may want to pause at this point to give an opportunity for children to talk about their initial feelings about the watertower. Some children may choose to write their own description of the watertower. Figures 5.2 and 5.3 show work from children in a year 4 and 5 class. They have decided to use their imagination and clues from the text to describe what it would be like to be inside the watertower.

Happenings at the watertower

The next pages are interesting as the text describes what Bubba is doing whereas in the illustrations we follow Spike running back to the town. Note in the double-page spread how the townsfolk are all staring in the direction of the watertower as if they are anticipating or waiting for something to happen. Read to the point where Bubba sees something move 'way up at the top of the tower'.

THE WATERTOWER

There in front of me was…

blackness — staring towards the tower, the burning sun had seared my sight — now there was nothing to be seen. Only in my mind could I visualise the horror of what had crawled out of the sun and enveloped the water—tower. In my last moments of ever being able to see again it had taken my sight — it might as well have taken my life.

Figure 5.3 Playing with possibilities

There, in front of me was … a monster? Spike? Both? A heart renching — something? My heart ached. I knew it was Spike, but it just … wasn't. It's eyes told me everything. Red, bolging, mysterious. Still. ~~He w~~ It was still. I was still. The world was still.

Figure 5.4 Creating intrigue and suspense

Ask the children what it could have been. Maybe suggest some possibilities indicating that it does not have to be a physical presence. Hand out some A5 paper and invite the children to draw what they think Bubba may have seen. You may want the children to add a caption to their picture in order to create a sense of mystery or suspense.

The next section leaves the reader with a multitude of questions to which there are no definite answers. Read the page where Bubba calls out to Spike, stands up and whispers Spike's name again. The next double page is a dramatic close up of Bubba's face. Show the double page to the children. Leave some time for them to take it in and then ask them what could have led Bubba to look like this? What has he seen? What is he thinking? What might he want to say?

Introduce the writing opportunity with the level of support needed for your class. In my experience, if the suspense has been built, the children do not need further ideas at this point and instead want to record their initial thoughts about what Bubba has seen. Give the opening phrase of 'There in front of him was . . .' and let children explore their own ideas through writing. I would suggest that adults in the classroom write as well, describing what they think Bubba may have seen. After a suitable period of time share some ideas and consider the effect of the writing on the reader. Which ideas leave questions in our minds and create curiosity? Figures 5.3 and 5.4 show the initial writing from children in year 6 responding to the intrigue created at this point in the story. You will be able to identify how the children have captured the sense of unknowing in their writing. Notice how in Figure 5.4 Parmjot uses ellipses, not because she had to or because it was on a list of success criteria but because she felt the *need* to in order to convey the meaning.

Figure 5.5 *The Watertower* display (Petworth C of E Primary School)

When it changed

The other day my life changed without warning. This secret I
do not want to tell to anyone and I hope that no one knows.
Something happened to me that made me change forever.

      I got out of the water tower and saw something
amazing behind the bush. It was ~~a kind of~~ glowing green,
and looked undescribably evil. For a while ~~the creat~~ I
just stood, astonished, staring at it. But then it spoke to
me. It said that I would never be free again, that I
would have to suffer for the rest of my life, never in
control of my own mind. I didn't understand. What and
was it saying?

      But suddenly I understood. I then found my
myself dlibing back up the ladder to the water tower,
I didn't want to do this, I didn't tell mysef to.
It did. It was controlling me, making me do what I
didn't want to. It had taken over me!
It continued to make me climb to the top of
the tower, then I found ~~myste~~ myself walking towards
the water. I knew exactly what was coming, but I
couldn't stop myself. I just kept walking to what I
thought would be death. Suddenly I stopped, lent forward
into the water and then, I fell. Straight into the
~~water darkness~~ surrounding darkness and underneath the
water. 1, 2, 3 I began to count. I counted all the
way up to 120. I was so worried but suddenly I
swam to the surface. I got out of the water and here
I saw my old friend. That was where everyones suspicion
begain...

      Now I do not have a life of my own. I live,
but not as myself. I am controlled by the creature. I am
never in control of my mind, never can do what I want,
never can think freely from the time when it changed

Figure 5.6 Bubba's diary

Concluding the drama

The next page may need rereading as it can be confusing. We move from what Bubba has seen to Bubba emerging from the watertower. I often talk with children about the fact that there must be a page missing or the pages must have stuck together. The mystery is what happened in between these two points. Children may want to return to their writing and continue their ideas leading to Bubba emerging from the watertower.

The final page contradicts what we are told earlier in the book and Bubba says his mother would be worried about him whereas at the beginning we are told that she could not have cared where he went. Children might note the mark of the watertower on Bubba's hand and may want to track back in the book or with the pictures you gave them at the start and identify all the places where the watertower has left its mark.

Make this your own

The Watertower is a story which often leaves the reader with more questions than answers. Some children may, at first, find this unsettling as they may possibly be used to stories where, at the end, all the loose ends have been tied up. However if we see a story as just one snapshot of a specific time and place we can start to understand that events took place before and will take place after the story. With this in mind you may want to work with the children exploring what the entries would be in the diaries of Spike and Bubba. Figure 5.6 shows an extract from Bubba's diary. Maybe the entries would be quite similar as they explored the town in which they lived but we know that for one event they would have very different accounts.

*

LITERATURE LINKS RELATING TO THE THEME

There are many other books which explore the theme of this chapter. You may want to use them to complement the work you are doing or see how some of the drama strategies will enable you to enrich the learning experience. Suitable recommendations for use with process drama include:

In the Wake of the Mary Celeste (2004, Thomas C. Lothian) by Gary Crew and Robert Ingpen

The Mystery of Eilean Mor (2005, Thomas C. Lothian) by Gary Crew and Jeremy Geddes

I am Thomas (2011, Allen and Unwin) by Libby Gleeson and illustrated by Armin Greder

Way Home (2003, Anderson Press) by Libby Hathorn and Gregory Rogers

The Widow's Broom (1992, Houghton Miffin Company) by Chris Van Allsburg

The Mysteries of Harris Burdick (2011, Anderson Press) by Chris Van Allsburg

The Coming of the Surfman (1993, Jonathan Cape) by Peter Collington.

6 Creative ideas with texts
Prejudice

In this section two texts will be used to explore issues surrounding notions of prejudice. We work on a daily basis to support our children, helping them understand themselves and others. The need to promote British values in schools has been on the government agenda, ensuring that every school promotes the basic British values of democracy, the rule of law, individual liberty, and mutual respect and tolerance for those of different faiths and beliefs. Those of us working in schools however know that this was happening anyway as part of our daily teaching, assemblies and the ethos of the school. However the texts chosen in this section will provide an opportunity to explore some of these values and will enable the reader to understand different characters' thoughts and feelings from within the situation they find themselves in.

THE GREEN CHILDREN (1997, OXFORD UNIVERSITY PRESS) BY KEVIN CROSSLEY-HOLLAND

- **Possible writing opportunity**: Letter writing
- **Interactive strategies**: Freeze-frame, thought tracking, improvisation, drawing in role, teacher in role (TiR), writing in role, hot seating
- **Age range**: 7–11

Introduction

The Green Children is an emotional text which touches on the themes of loss, community, relationships and fitting into a society. We meet the green children on the first page as they have stumbled across a new world which is unfamiliar to them. The sky is different, the trees are different and most significantly the people are different. A family takes them in and looks after them to the best of their ability but the green children are always longing for home. At an emotional point in the story the younger child becomes ill and 'the song went out of him'. Feeling even more isolated we understand the need for the girl to integrate more within the society. However her experience at the fair causes her to run away with the echoes, jeers and taunts ringing in her ears.

The story is originally a folk tale dating back to 1135. The story is of two children who were found in the village of Woolpit in Suffolk. The children emerged from the deep ditches made in order to trap wolves. They had a green tint to their skin and wore clothes which were unfamiliar to the villagers. More information can be accessed at: http://brian-haughton.com/ancient-mysteries-articles/green-children-of-woolpit/.

Teaching objectives

- Develop willingness to accept and respect the ideas of others and to build on them.
- Identify with characters and actions through role playing.
- Realise that the views of individuals do not always coincide.
- Explore the differences between right and wrong in simple moral dilemmas posed through drama.
- Contribute ideas through using the imagination

Problems, emotions or challenges to be explored

- The first problem for the children is how to get home. They have arrived in an area unfamiliar to them and know that their own parents will be worried.
- The second problem is when the younger of the children dies. The green girl will feel remorse, guilt and responsibility.
- The third issue is at the point where the green girl enters the fair. She is excited and looking forward to the fair only to be taunted, jeered at and ridiculed.

The session

The ideas presented are intended to be adapted and shaped by you for use in your class. They are not intended as a formula to follow or as a lesson plan. You may feel that you would like, for example, to take one idea and expand on it depending on the interests of your class or you may want to sequence a few of the ideas together. The text should help inspire teaching with a purpose which creates passion and empowers the class. This will depend, not only on the interests of your class, but also on your characteristics as a teacher. Some ideas will resonate more strongly with you than others. I hope the ideas you do use and embellish will mean that your class encounters imaginative teaching with purpose and passion for empowerment.

Connecting with the theme

Display a picture depicting a character feeling isolated and alone. You could search online for a suitable picture. Invite children to comment on the character's thoughts and feelings. Ask them how we know what they are feeling. Look at the body language and facial expressions. Predict what the situation may have been leading to the character feeling like this.

Discuss with the children whether the picture resonates with them and whether they have ever felt alone. In small groups or pairs give opportunities for children to share their experiences. Aim also to share one of your own experiences with the children so they can see that these issues touch all our lives. Draw connections between the common elements within the stories being shared. Themes may include: moving to a new house/school, friendship issues, not sharing the same interests as others.

Introducing the text

Display the front cover of the text *The Green Children*. Make sure all children have time to look at the picture and discuss their initial reactions.

After allowing children time, in small groups, to discuss the front cover encourage a discussion based on their initial thoughts about the text. Conversations may include talk about the differences between the two sets of children, where the story might take place, what the relationship might be between the two green children and what each of the other children might be thinking.

First encounters

Start to read the first page up to the point where it says 'When my brother and I opened our eyes, we saw faces peering down at us'. This is a potentially tense point within the story as we do not know how either the green children or the other children will react. We can explore this through the use of a freeze-frame to depict the moment when the green children opened their eyes and saw the other children peering down at them.

Invite the children to form groups of about five. Within the group, children should decide who will take the role of the green children and who will be the other children. As a group, discuss what the responses might be from each character. What might they say as they encounter children who are green and how might the green children react? After a brief discussion count down from five to zero at which point each group should freeze in their freeze-frame. Encourage the groups to use their bodies as the description. They should think about how their stance, facial expression and body actions will serve to describe this potentially tense moment in the text.

With the children in their freeze-frames, storytell this moment in the text where the green children are being stared at by the other children. You do not need to use the printed text but instead spontaneously narrate the situation as you will want to create space to explore the thoughts and feelings of both sets of children. Therefore, as you tell the story weave in points where you have opportunities to hear the voices of both the green children and the other children in this, their first encounter. Choose some children to speak their thoughts by tapping them on the shoulder to indicate they should share a thought or feeling in role as their character. Continue the narrative and invite the other children to participate with their thoughts and feelings.

In the same small groups invite the children to think of a caption which summarises their freeze-frames. Examples may include: Lost and alone, A new land, No escape, Friend or foe. Take some time, if appropriate, to look at each of the freeze-frame and hear the captions. Discuss which captions capture the mood of the story at this point.

Extending the drama

Continue reading the text from the first page. Discuss with the children why phrases such as 'he bumped his bottom and his brains', 'they forefingered us', 'they hissed behind their hands' are used. Extrapolate the fact that the story is from the girl's point of view so she is explaining in literal terms what she sees. Explore with the children what other day-to-day actions might be described in other ways.

Continue reading to the point where it says 'The children walked us through a creaking wood'. Create the imagined scene in the classroom. Tell the children that they are the green boy or girl. Invite them to walk around the classroom looking in awe at the beauty and difference in their surroundings. Explain that you want the children to notice three things which are different. Once they have noticed something they should go and find another green child to tell them what they have noticed. Alternatively you could clap your hands indicating that children should stop and then tell the child closest to them what they have noticed.

Continue by asking the children to walk with you while you narrate what you have seen in the surroundings. Occasionally stop to look at something closely. During one of the pauses encourage the children to stop and to fix their eyes on something they have noticed: something curious, something they have not seen before. Ask them to slowly reach out and pick their item up. It could be a leaf, a twig, a minibeast or possibly bark from a tree. Ask children to feel their object. Ask open-ended questions as the children explore their object – something they, as the green child, have never seen before.

Ask the children to carefully take their imagined object back to their tables. You may now want them to draw or possibly make the object. Once drawn or made explain that as the green child you want to take the object back to your homeland . . . but how would you describe it? Model how to describe one of the objects. It works well if this is an object which you have drawn which you can show the class. Talk with the class about why you picked this object and discuss your thought process while drawing it. Then describe how you would describe it to your family. In the past the following descriptions have been generated by children:

Object in our world	Description by one of the green children
Leaf	It's so flat and light. It looks as though it has a skeleton. I wonder if it is alive.
Twig	The outer shell seems to flake away leaving the inner part exposed. Maybe it will grow a new shell.
Woodlouse	It moves . . . really fast! And tickles when on my hand.
Stone	There is no start and no end. I don't know how to open it. It is really hard and heavy.
Flower	So beautiful! It seems so precious and delicate in an array of different colours.

Invite children to discuss then write the description of their object. Figure 6.1 shows how Katherine chose to describe a flower she picked up in the forest. They should imagine they are describing the object to their parents who will never have seen anything like this before. You could display the objects and the descriptions in a museum style.

It was soft and fragile with many layers. But the colour was different to us and it had lots of different colours.

Figure 6.1 Describing a flower from the forest

Trying to return home

Continue reading to the point where it says 'the dark light almost took our eyes from us'. Ask the children to discuss how they would feel if they had not experienced darkness before. What would the green children think is happening? You could use the thought-tracking technique here to find out what the green children would be thinking. Circulate around the classroom narrating the story intermittently tapping a child on the shoulder in order to weave in their thoughts.

At this point in the story the green children will be feeling lost and alone in a strange land. The text does not tell us specifically how they are feeling or what they might say so the next drama convention helps us connect our own experiences to those of the green children and voice their thoughts.

Organise the children by asking them to form a circle in the classroom around a chair. The chair is simply the focal point for the drama and represents the green children. This will be an opportunity for the children to voice the worries or concerns experienced by the green children. Model how to step from the circle and touch the chair before voicing one thought from a green child. You may say, for example 'I wish we never found our way to this land. All I want to do is go home' or 'This land is so strange. Nothing is like home. I want to go now.' Then invite children, when they are ready, to follow your lead and share their thought at this time in role as a green child.

If possible while the sharing is taking place ask another adult to scribe some of the thoughts being shared on the flipchart or large paper. Some children may want to record their thoughts at this point as shown in Figure 6.2.

> I don't know if I'll ever be able to see my parents again. I'm so scared I don't know what happened. I don't want to live here, I want to go back, to my world. What's goiong on? I don't like it here, I'm scared, everything is different. I want to go back. Will I ever be able to get back? It's gone, everything gone.
>
> I will get us back, we will find a way home! I'm so sorry, it's all my fault. I love you. please don't go. Don't go, don't leave me.

(handwritten insertion above: "whatever happens")

Figure 6.2 Yearning for their own land

Creating tensions and conflict

As children return to their seats continue reading from the text. If the text is being displayed for the class to see, note the significance of the white space before and after the line 'After seven days my brother felt ill'. At the end of the page narrate the thoughts and feelings of the girl at this moment. Explain how she gently lay her brother down and spoke to him. She spoke of her regret, her responsibility and her wishes. As a whole class discuss what some of these would be. Tell the class that as a way of reconciliation the green girl felt compelled to write to her parents to explain what had happened.

Use the ideas from the flipchart as well as ideas from the discussion to form the letter the green girl would write. Children could maybe work individually or in pairs to form the letter. During the writing process it may be appropriate to play some suitable atmospheric music.

Explain that the green girl decides to leave the letter with her brother. Once the letters have been written invite the children to come up and symbolically place the letter on the chair which represents her brother.

Feeling accepted then rejected

Continue reading to the point in the text where it says 'I'll come, I said.' With the children discuss what sort of sights and sounds might be at a carnival or a fair. The list may include people selling a range of products including sweets, fruit and crafts. Others features may include people entertaining with juggling, dancing and acrobatics. The aim will be to create the scene in the classroom. Assign children roles and build up the atmosphere of the fair. Other children take on the role of the green child. Allow them to intermingle exploring the delights on offer. On your signal of 'Freeze one' the first set of children creating the fair will freeze allowing the green children to walk from stall to stall tasting, touching and exploring. There will also have been a dramatic decrease in sound.

At your command of 'Freeze all' the green children will also freeze leaving you the opportunity to hear their thoughts by tapping a selection of the green children on the shoulder. A sense of excitement, awe and wonder would have built up as this is the first fair the green child has been to.

Narrate the next part of the story referring to the text noting that the fair did not develop in that way. Instead the girl was taunted, jeered and ridiculed. Read or narrate the story to the point where it says 'She's a freak! They screamed. She's green!'

Narrate the story, moving away from the specifics in the text. Narrate that she turned and ran, ran as fast as she could away from this place. Scenes from the last month flashed through her head and she worked out that she was not welcome in this place. She ran to Guy's house, a place she had been trying to call home. Going inside she grabbed the paper and wrote her final letter to Alice, Guy and the family. Explaining her thoughts and feelings and saying that she knows that she is not welcome in this world. Figure 6.3 shows one letter written by a child in year 5 who was writing in role after the drama.

> Dear Alice
>
> Indeed I was, buzzing with antisipation, when you told me about the fare. I thought it'd be amazin, with people having fun and laughing. They were laughing. At me. Infact, not only laughing, they were pointing, shouting, and jeering at me. My heart was torn to shreds. Maybe they had never seen a green person before, but I'd not seen black, brown and white skins before either. When I witnessed it, I did not laugh, or hide or jeer. But they did. My brother has died, and I am lost, and all alone in this place. I have got to leave. I am not one of you, and I never will be. I am one of a kind. Though I truly wish I wasn't. I cannot live like this. I am sorry. I shall go and live in a forest, with trees and grass, and colours so greet, they'd understand me. Though thank you.

Figure 6.3 The letter to the family

Allow children time to write their letter, scaffolding as appropriate. Ensure the scaffolding does not get in the way of the emotive voice. Give out envelopes and children address it as appropriate. For example they may write 'My dearest Guy'.

Once the letters have been written explain that the green girl left the letter on the side for Guy and then left the house. At this point narrate that Guy comes running into the house picks up the letter and reads it. As TiR, read the letter as Guy. At different points within your reading of the letter respond as Guy maybe with surprise and sorrow at what has been written.

Explain that after reading the letter Guy really needs to talk with the green girl and so goes out to find her. Guy finds the green girl in the woods at the same point where she entered this strange world. Invite some children to be in role as the green girl to answer questions from Guy. Give the rest of the children time to think of some questions they may want to ask as Guy. Initially role play the situation either in groups or as a whole class before using the hot-seat technique to explore the thoughts and feelings of the green girl in more detail.

Concluding the drama

Return to the text reading the last few pages. Encourage the children in groups to discuss the themes and significant moments in the text. Which points resonated most closely with them and why? Are there any similarities to other texts they have encountered?

Provide groups with a range of collage material of various forms and colours. Working in small groups children have the task of depicting what they believe the meaning of the story is for them through the materials.

Make this your own

You could take one theme from the text and explore that in more detail. For example you could look for ways in which the green children could get home. Imagine that they did find a way home how would they convince their family and friends that they had found a new world. Maybe they would be able to convince some of them to come back to the new world with them.

You could link the work in this text to work you are already doing in subjects such as PSHE or RE focusing on similarities and differences, bullying and racism.

*

THE ISLAND (2008, ALLEN & UNWIN) BY ARMIN GREDER

- **Possible writing opportunities**: Newspaper account

- **Interactive strategies**: Role of the wall, improvisation, decision alley, role play, freeze-frame, group tableaux

- **Age range**: 9–11

Introduction

This book expertly deals with issues of prejudice, misrepresentation, misunderstanding, fear of the unknown and isolation. With the heightened awareness of issues relating to the travels by refugees into mainland Europe this text will serve as a way of exploring these issues and providing opportunities for discussion. *The Island* was the first book in which Armin Greder contributed both the visual and written text, something he repeated in his book *The City*.

The illustrations are striking in their depiction of the events taking place on the island and time should be given for detailed exploration of them throughout the work on this text. The story is about a man who is found on the beach of *The Island* but he was not like the islanders. Initial puzzlement and islanders questioning the reasons why he had come to the island were answered by the conscience of the fisherman who decided they should take him in. However as time went on rumours and suspicion grew and spread resulting in the islanders seizing the man and pushing him back out to sea before building a fortress around the island to protect themselves and to ensure no one ever found their island again.

Teaching objectives

- Develop willingness to accept and respect the ideas of others and to build on them.

- Have the confidence and ability to put across a particular point of view.

- Realise that the views of individuals do not always coincide.

- Learn how to work together to solve human and practical problems.

- Contribute ideas through using the imagination.

- Create and take part in improvised scenes in order to explore particular issues which could, for instance, have a practical, social or moral dimension.

Problems, emotions or challenges to be explored

- The first issue relates to the notion of belonging. How many different groups do we belong to? We can think of this in terms of a hierarchical approach starting with the human race as a group we all belong to but what are the benefits and dangers of finding ourselves part of and associated with sub-groups?

- The second issue explores the idea of the fear of the unknown. This is a powerful theme and will give the children the opportunity to speak openly about feeling they have about people and places they do not have an understanding of. How does this affect their judgement?

- The third issue relates to the instances when rumours and gossip come in the way of facts.

The session

The ideas presented are intended to be adapted and shaped by you for use in your class. They are not intended as a formula to follow or as a lesson plan. You may feel that you would like, for example, to take one idea and expand on it depending on the interests of your class or you may want to sequence a few of the ideas together. The text should help inspire teaching with a purpose which creates passion and empowers the class. This will depend, not only on the interests of your class, but also on your characteristics as a teacher. Some ideas will resonate more strongly with you than others. I hope the ideas you do use and embellish will mean that your class encounters imaginative teaching with purpose and passion for empowerment.

Connecting with the setting

Ask the children what their perception of an island is? What other books, films, pictures, adverts and videos can they think of in which an island features? Ask the children to imagine an island in their mind. Talk them through imagining that they are standing on the island.

What can you see?	Look around you, what do you notice? Are there any trees, any people, any buildings? Look at the ground. What is it like? Is it different to what you are used to? Look into the distance, as far as you can. What do you see? What colours can you see? Can you describe them?
What can you hear?	Listen carefully, can you hear the sea? What does it sound like? How does it make you feel? Does the sound bring back any memories for you? What other sounds can you hear?
What can you touch?	Reach down to the ground. What does the surface feel like? Is it hot or cold? What is the texture like?
What can you taste and smell?	Breathe in and take a moment to consider what the smell reminds you of. Is it a sweet pleasant smell? Is it overpowering?
How do you feel?	As you stand on the island what feelings do you have? Are you feeling rested, reassured and relaxed? Do you have any concerns or worries?

At this point you could ask the children to draw their imagined island. Discuss with them the features they would put on their island. Discuss with the children what they could name their island and how this represents the uniqueness of their own island. Explain that we will contract and compare their islands with the one depicted in the text.

Introducing the text

Introduce the front cover of the text to the children. Does the picture surprise them in any way? Ask the children what title would better represent the picture? They may think of titles such as 'The Fortress', 'The Castle' or 'The Tower' among others. Some children may refer to the picture and comment that it could be a sandcastle on the beach of an island.

Show the children the title page and give the children an opportunity to explore what the picture shows. Children will soon notice the raft in the foreground of the picture. Ask a series of questions to highlight the possibilities such as: Where might the raft be heading? Who could be on the raft? Why might they be on the raft?

Talk about whether being on the raft is a safe place to be. Note down reasons why it might be safe and why it might not be safe. Move the conversation on to explore places where the children feel safe and the reasons for that. They may talk about familiarity of location, people and objects in their answers. Gather the responses and refer back to them as the text progresses.

First encounters

Read the first page. Take time to look at the various possible interpretations of the first three lines. For example discuss what the author may mean by 'fate'? Then show the picture of the man and the text 'He wasn't like them'. The amount of white space between the three lines and the final line is interesting. Talk to the children about what this might depict and why the author left this space. Discuss in what ways the man might be different. Draw an outline of the man on large paper and encourage children to contemplate the physical and emotional ways in which he may differ from the people of the island. After initial discussions in groups children could use sticky notes to write down their ideas and come and stick physical differences around the outside of the outline and emotional differences inside the outline. This activity will raise the awareness of the ways in which people can be different in the context of seen and unseen differences.

Explain that we have all seen the man who arrived on the raft and now we are going to look at the islanders. Pair or group the children and give one child in the pair or group the picture of the next two pages which shows the islanders. Their task is to describe it in as much detail as they can to their partner or the rest of the group who need to listen carefully for any key words the describer uses. They may want to draw what they imagine the picture to be or to jot down key words and phrases. Before showing the rest of the class the image, bring the class back together and ask for feedback relating to the key words used.

Return to the outline of the man and, using different colour sticky notes, add any differences which can be ascertained from the text. Ask the children whether there are any previous comments which can now be removed. Children may find that they are predominantly changing the physical characteristics but the emotional characteristic may stay the same. Discuss the possible reasons for this and whether they feel that, as the text continues, they will find out more about the differing emotional features of the man and the islanders.

Conflicting thoughts

Read the text which accompanies the picture of the group of islanders which is the first evidence of a disagreement between them concerning what they should do with the man. The main group want to send the man away whereas the fisherman, who knew the dangers of the sea, wanted the man to stay. Ask the children to take the role of either the fisherman or one of the islanders. Explain that we are going to explore their thoughts at this point in the story concerning what they think should happen to the man and why. Invite the class to form a thought tunnel. Choose one child to be in role as the man who will walk through the tunnel and listen to the views of the islanders. It is of course important to choose the child carefully. The class should be used to being in role and taking part in drama activities before this specific drama activity is used.

Read the next page where we are told that 'they took him in'. This is a fascinating picture which exposes the differing power relations between the islanders and the man. Explore what thoughts might be going through the man's mind. In the picture he looks resigned to his fate, powerless and defenceless before the islanders but also in a sense trusting of what might happen to him. Children could use thought bubbles to interrogate this narrative in more detail. Alternatively you could set the scene up in the classroom with children recreating this picture through a freeze-frame. Then invite other class members to come up, touch the man or one of the islanders on the shoulder and speak his thoughts at this moment in the text.

Read the next page in which the islanders take the man to an uninhabited part of the Island. We are told that 'They made him understand that he was to stay there'. Why has the author chosen these words? Discuss with the class what this may have looked like. Exemplify the differences and difficulties that language barriers may present for some people and how these can be overcome. This reinforces the theme throughout the book regarding similarities and differences. Children can discuss that although the spoken language may be different there will be universal signs, symbols and expressions which will be the same. The pictures on this double page are interesting as they depict 'life as normal' on the island. The four portrait pictures imply an imbalance in gender equality whereas the picture at the bottom of the page gives us an insight into how prejudices can be copied, learned and re-enacted.

Escaping from captivity

The next picture depicts how the islanders felt when they saw the man in the town. Children may want to explore the events leading up to the man appearing in the town. How and why did the man leave the locked goat pen? How much time had passed between him being locked up and appearing in the town? There are gaps to be filled in the text in which children can explore a range of possibilities. One idea, after initial discussions, is to invite children in small groups to produce a freeze-frame of the moment the man escaped from the pen. The freeze-frame should let the viewer know how he escaped. Some children may think that a long time had passed and he dug a tunnel, others may think that he smashed the surrounding wall down, groups may think that he built a ladder out of odd bits of wood – the possibilities are endless. Count down from five to zero with the expectations that the groups will freeze into their positions on zero. While all the children are in their freeze-frames explain that you will go around the freeze-frames and when you touch the man on the shoulder he should say what he is thinking and feeling at this time. You may need to support the children by giving some examples or posing questions.

Return to the powerful picture of the islander. If possible provide each pair or group with a copy of the picture and ask them to note down how the islander feels, how she would make other people feel and how the illustrator achieves this.

Continue reading to the point where the islanders are suggesting jobs for the man, and excuses and reservations are voiced giving reasons why he would be unsuitable. Ask the children what other jobs could he be asked to undertake? Once you have generated a range of responses invite the children to form pairs. Each child needs to take on the role of the proprietor of one of the jobs. Ask the children to think of reasons why the man would not be able to work for them. Then set the scene in the class explaining that rumours and gossip were spreading about the fact that the fisherman has suggested that one of us gives the man a job. As the islanders went about their business discussions, turn to reasons why the man could not work for them. At this point children should, in paired role, explain to each other their reasons. After a short period of time stop the children and ask them to feedback some of the responses. These could be noted on a flipchart. Discuss which responses were the most effective and why. Look at the language features and the effect they have on the listener. Explain that other islanders had overheard their conversations and came to join in. Ask the children to form groups of four to represent the growing group of islanders concerned about the prospect of the man working for them. Some children may wish to refer to the effective examples on the flipchart as they, in groups of four, repeat the role play. Depending on your class this activity could develop until you have large groups of islanders (maybe three groups of ten) partaking in the role play.

Continue reading the text and showing and responding to the pictures until the point where we are told 'I am sure that he would murder us all if he could'. There is an opportunity at this point to reflect on the story so far and to imagine what the headline might be in the newspaper the next day. The previous seven portrait pictures could be used for this activity to stimulate discussions regarding the possible stories.

Creating stories

Ask children, in small 'story groups', to consider what the story and head-line could be. Give enough opportunity for the children to talk about the possibilities, refining and shaping their ideas with the aim of thinking of a headline which summarises their thoughts and attracts interest. After initial discussions children should write their headline on folded A4 card and display it on their tables.

Split the class into two groups. Group one should sit at their tables in their 'story groups' and display their headline ready to tell the story behind the headline. The other half of the class has time to walk around the classroom looking at the headlines. On your signal they should choose a headline which sparks their curiosity and go and sit at the table ready to hear the story. Children in the each story group will then tell their story to the other children. This can be repeated a couple of times so children can see that their stories will evolve with retelling before swapping the groups over.

Once children have heard a range of stories and told their own story you could develop this into newspaper writing by setting your class up with children taking on the various roles within the newspaper industry. Children could be reporters, journalists, photographers, editors and publishers. Careful planning would ensure that the aim of producing a range of front pages involves all children and develops the initial stories they told.

Concluding the drama

Return to the text and read to the end of the story where the villages capture the man, tie him up and push him back on his raft before setting fire to the fisherman's boat and building a wall around the island. Ask the children, as a whole class to form the wall around the island. They may want to link arms and face outwards. Once they have formed the wall surrounding the island ask them to think about what the wall represents. Children may want to think about what the wall represents from the islanders' point of view or from the point of view of someone trying to access the island. Give some ideas yourself before walking around the outside of the wall and tapping selected children on the shoulder to hear what they have to say.

Then look at the situation from the man's point of view. Tell the children to imagine that they are the man on his raft and have just been pushed out to sea. Ask the children to find their own space in the room and imagine they are moving further and further away from the island. What would his thoughts be at this time? Would he be relieved to be away from the island? Maybe he would be confused about his treatment or possibly he could be reflecting on what his actual intentions were when on the island. Children could respond in a number of ways. You could use thought tracking or you may prefer to con-tinue the idea of silence which was a feature of the man's time on the island. Within the text we did not hear his words or his thoughts. You may wish therefore for the children to use thought bubbles and to write what they think the man could be thinking before coming to stick it on an outline of the man displayed in the classroom.

Reflect with the children what they consider the themes of the text are. They may come up with themes such as: fear, prejudice, discrimination, anger, peer pressure or isolation, among many others. In small groups ask the children to represent what they feel the story is about through a group tableaux.

Make this your own

You could use this story in relation to the migrant crisis in Europe which attracted significant attention in 2015. A collection of newspaper reports from this time could be shown to the children as well as the different approaches adopted by the European governments. On a smaller scale you may want to relate the story to new people joining the class and the school and discussing how we should treat them and welcome them.

*

LITERATURE LINKS RELATING TO THIS THEME

There are many other books which explore the theme of this chapter. You may want to use them to complement the work you are doing or see how some of the drama strategies will enable you to enrich the learning experience. Suitable recommendations for use with process drama include:

A Bad Case of Stripes (1998, Scholastic) by David Shannon

The Colour of Home (2002, Frances Lincoln) by Mary Hoffman

The Bird Man (2000, Anderson) by Melvin Burgess

Rose Blanche (2004, Red Fox) by Roberto Innocenti and Ian McEwan

Erika's Story (2004, Random House) by Ruth Vander Zee and Roberto Innocenti

The Savage (2008, Walker) by David Almond

The Heart in the Bottle (2007, Harper) by Oliver Jeffers

The Two Frogs (2003, Jonathan Cape) by Chris Wormell

Luba, the Angel of Bergen Belsen (2003, Adams) by Michelle McCann, Luba Tryszynska-Frederick and Ann Marshall.

7 Creative ideas with texts
Friendship

This section includes a range of suggestions for discussing the topic of friendship. The texts identified can be used in the classroom to help children explore the questions of who are our friends, what are the characteristics of a friend and should we be a friend to all people? Working through the texts elaborated on here or through the texts within the literature links, children can have the opportunity to talk about their own friendships as well as the friendships of the characters within the stories. This section could complement work as part of the Personal, Social and Health Education (PSHE) or could contribute towards work on British values.

ROSE MEETS MR WINTERGARTEN (2003, WALKER BOOKS) BY BOB GRAHAM

- **Possible writing opportunities**: Newspaper account, letter writing
- **Interactive strategies**: Role play, drawing, decision alley, forum theatre, group sculpture
- **Age range**: 3–7 (can also be used in Key Stage Two)

Introduction

This is a story about friendship, trust, prejudice and isolation. In it we meet Rose and her family who have just moved into their new neighbourhood. It seems to be an ordinary neighbourhood except for the presence of a large house with barbed wire lining the boundary and an overgrown garden of cacti and other uninviting plants. Stories are rife about the house and the man who lives there – Mr Wintergarten!

We know that it is inevitable that Rose will be put in a situation where she needs to confront Mr Wintergarten and this happens when her ball goes over his fence and she is tasked with the responsibility of retrieving it. Bravely, Rose makes her way to Mr Wintergarten's door and enters the house where she sees him sitting at a large table eating some uninviting food. His character at this point matches the uninviting nature of his food and, although Rose asks politely for her ball, she is told to leave the house.

However, simply the presence of Rose within Mr Wintergarten's house and the fact that Rose had actually asked him for her ball causes him to realise that he had been unreasonable and a change stirs in his spirit. Opening the curtains for the first time in years allows the sunlight to swallow up the darkness and frees Mr Wintergarten from the issues he had been dealing with.

The story concludes with a double-page picture showing Mr Wintergarten playing football and the garden which had engulfed his house for so many years being re-landscaped.

Teaching objectives

- Understand and take pleasure in the difference between pretence and reality.
- Contribute ideas through using the imagination.
- Have the confidence and ability to put across a particular point of view.
- Explore the differences between right and wrong in simple moral dilemmas posed through drama.
- Explore the variety of human emotions.
- Identify with characters and actions through role-playing.

Problems, emotions or challenges to be explored

- The first issue is concerned with how rumours and gossip can spread causing distortions of the truth.
- The second issue relates to the idea of 'stranger danger' and whether Rose should, in reality, enter Mr Wintergarten's house.
- The final issue explores the reasons why Mr Wintergarten kept himself away from the community for such a long period of time.

The session

The ideas presented are intended to be adapted and shaped by you for use in your class. They are not intended as a formula to follow or as a lesson plan. You may feel that you would like, for example, to take one idea and expand on it depending on the interests of your class or you may want to sequence a few of the ideas together. The text should help inspire teaching with a purpose which creates passion and empowers the class. This will depend, not only on the interests of your class, but also on your characteristics as a teacher. Some ideas will resonate more strongly with you than others. I hope the ideas you do use and embellish will mean that your class encounters imaginative teaching with purpose and passion for empowerment.

Connecting with the theme

Before sharing the book you may want to discuss with the children if any of them have experienced moving house. Give time for a discussion exploring the issues of excitement, anticipation, problems encountered and making friends.

Introducing the text

This text starts with a brilliant double-page spread in which the majority of the space is taken up with an imposing and ominous house where Bob Graham uses colours which at first glance appear to be grey and gloomy, but on closer inspection we can see that there are shades of yellow in the picture. The use of colour and the images they conjure up is an important discussion to have with the children. To me the yellowish grey represents an old, faded and forgotten newspaper which may have been important in its day but now is discarded by the reader without any care or attention. In contrast the smaller house is depicted with a range of homely, bright colours. Your discussion about the page may include looking at some of the characters and considering who they are, what they might be thinking and what they might say.

Generating stories

Read the first four pages with the children, pausing to concentrate on the picture on pages 3 and 4 which show the children sitting on the roof of their house watching the sun come up. Explain that the children had heard stories about Mr Wintergarten, stories which may be true or could possibly have been made up. As they sit on the roof the conversation changes to stories they had heard about Mr Wintergarten, stories they knew were fact and stories they knew were fiction but all stories which made them think, consider and wonder . . . At this point improvise by giving some examples of what they may have heard. Invite the children to come up with their own story and in role as one of the children on the roof to share it with their partner.

Explain that these stories were soon all around the town and people were talking about them as they queued in the grocer's, as they walked their dogs and as they came out of church on Sunday. Invite the children to stand up and push their chairs in. Use the space in the classroom to depict the alleyways, roads and thoroughfares of the village. They will be in role as the villagers may be heading home or walking to the shops. Encourage children to walk around the classroom until you clap your hands. On that signal they should go to the closest person and tell them the story they have heard about Mr Wintergarten. You could possibly repeat the process about three times.

First imaginings

Read the next two pages where we hear some of the other stories shared about Mr Wintergarten. Tell the class that the conversations move on to what Mr Wintergarten might look like. As you talk, invite the children to build an image of Mr Wintergaten in their heads. Ask open questions, elaborating on some of them in order to support children's mental image making. How tall is he? How old is he? What type of clothes does he wear? What do his hands look like? You could encourage the children to imagine that they are Mr Wintergarten and ask them to walk in his style, to pick up a bowl in his style and to sit down in his style.

Hand out some A5 paper and ask the children to draw what they think Mr Wintergarten might look like. Figures 7.1 and 7.2 show the initial thoughts of what children in year 3 thought Mr Wintergarten might look like. If possible you could also draw your depiction of Mr Wintergarten. It would be interesting

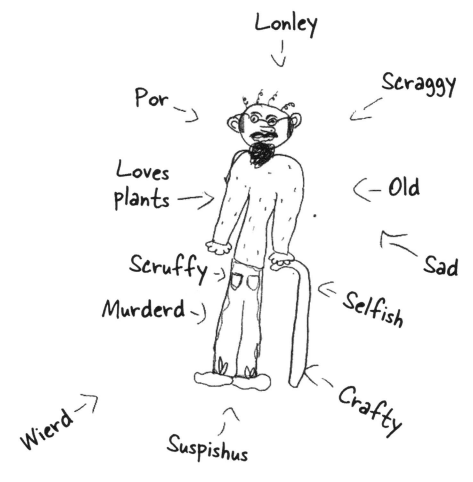

Lonley

Por

Scraggy

Loves plants

Old

Scruffy

Sad

Murderd

Selfish

Wierd

Crafty

Suspishus

Figure 7.1 Imagining what Mr Wintergarten might look like

to note the similarities and differences in the drawings taking place. After a suitable length of time, while the children are drawing, offer a choice. Invite children to either add some words to describe Mr Wintergarten or ask them to imagine that their picture was in fact on the front page of the local newspaper 10 years ago but what was the headline? Ask the children to think about what the headline could have been and add it to their picture.

Conflicting thoughts

At this point you could seize the moment and work with the headlines the children have thought of. This would depend on whether you can sense a feeling of excitement, intrigue and anticipation about the headlines (not because it could lead to report writing!). Start to question some of the events which could have led up to the headlines in order to encourage children to think about the background to their stories. Depending on the responses you could then work on fleshing out the range of intriguing stories relating to the headlines. At this point you may want to put the children into small groups in role as competing

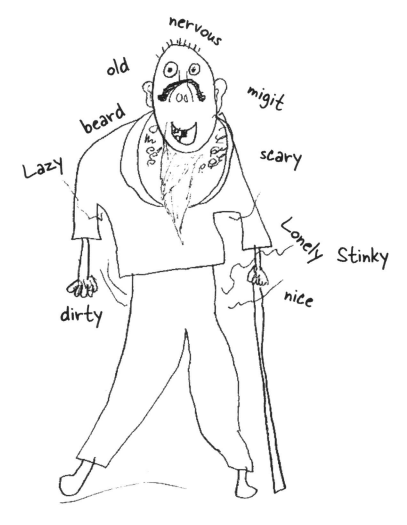

Figure 7.2 Imagining what Mr Wintergarten might look like

newspaper proprietors. In their groups the children are tasked with producing the front page for their newspaper.

Alternatively you could continue with the story and read to the point where Rose's ball goes straight over Mr Wintergarten's fence. Here Rose has a dilemma. Where she used to live Rose would go round to her neighbours and ask for her ball back but in this neighbourhood, with all the stories she has heard, Rose is unsure of what to do. At this point in the text we can use the drama convention of 'conscience corridor' or 'decision alley' to explore the conflict within Rose's head. Invite the children to form two lines for Rose to walk through. The children need to be ready to voice what they consider Rose may be thinking. You also need to choose a child to be Rose and to walk the length of the alley listening to the conflicting thoughts in her own mind. It may be tempting to try to encourage each child to think of something 'different' but in reality the thoughts in our minds which, at times, are most persuasive or dominant are those which seem to repeat themselves over and over again.

Once the child in role as Rose has walked down the corridor ask the other children to sit down and give Rose some time to consider what her course of action would be based on what she has heard. As the teacher it is important here to honour the decision Rose makes and is another example of where you may need to 'seize the moment'. There are a myriad of options Rose could decide on, for example she could decide to jump over the fence to get her ball, she may simply go and buy a new ball or maybe she wants to ask Mr Wintergarten for her ball back. You need to be ready to respond in an authentic way to whatever decision Rose comes to. For example if she decides to just leave the ball you will need to weave this into the story. You could say 'As she passes the fence each day and sees her ball just lying there she knows she has done the right thing – who needs an old football anyway? Her curiosity was aroused however when, on her normal route to meet her friends, she glanced into the garden and her ball was . . . gone. She knew that no one would have gone into the garden to retrieve it and so the only person who could have taken it was – Mr Wintergarten. Now she was going to meet him!'

Developing the drama

Alternatively if Rose decides to get the ball or to seek further advice you can continue with the story to where eventually Rose is standing at the gate of Mr Wintergarten's grounds looking towards the house. It is worth considering the many different senses Rose would be experiencing here. You can do that by creating a 'sense splat'. Depending on the class this could be an individual, group or class activity. If you decide on a whole-class activity put flipchart or large paper around the classroom with pictures depicting the senses of what Rose would see, hear, smell, taste, touch and feel (emotions). Put a variety of sticky notes on each table and, after returning to the picture in the book, encourage children to think about suitable words and phrases to describe the senses Rose is experiencing. After a short period of time stop the children and share some of the ideas they have come up with. Model how you can expand one-word responses into phrases and discuss how using a phrase will enable the writing process later to be easier.

Allow children time to continue using the sticky notes to record their ideas. Children will then put the notes from their tables on to the correct 'sense' around the classroom. At this point, model how you can use the ideas from the senses to start to write a descriptive piece about Rose's walk towards Mr Wintergarten's door. The modelling process is important and I would encourage you to do it spontaneously as this will be authentic writing rather than pre-planned writing. Once you have modelled the writing for the children give them time either individually or in groups to write their description. You could then ask children to read their work out while re-enacting Rose's walk to the door! Figure 7.3 shows the shared writing created with a group of children from year 4.

Rose's walk!

Rose stood staring at the rusty iron gates, the hairs on the back of her neck stood up and she could hear the rapid beat of her heart against her chest. Rose took a deep breath, counted to ten and slowly moved towards the gate. With a trembling hand she pushed and the gate creaked with a weathered sigh. Rose stepped through the gap into the wilderness that was Mr Wintergarten's garden. Like wilting statues, the once tall trees and bushes curled their heads downwards almost as if they were watching the little girl's every move. Rose could feel her unsteady breathing and had to stop herself from turning back, running back through those gates and forgetting all about the stupid ball. "Why ever did I volunteer to get the ball?" whirled around her mind, but her conscience prickled and she knew she was being silly. Mr Wintergarten couldn't possibly be that bad, could he? After all it seemed as if nobody in town had actually seen him for years and with his garden so overgrown he had obviously not stepped foot out of the big house for a long time too. Rose paused on the stone path to catch her breath. As she looked down at her feet it seemed as if the weeds were clinging even tighter in the vain hope of stopping her walk up to the big wooden door. But with every step Rose's determination was growing and her need to find out the truth about Mr Wintergarten kept her feet firmly on the path.

Figure 7.3 Shared writing of Rose's walk

My dearest Wilfred,

If you are reading this then... well you know the rest don't you. Sometimes dearest Wilfred we are unable to face the pain, face the disappointment, the heartache and the misery. I always knew that you had the resolve to cope and this is a time when you need to – I know it only too well.

Wilfred remember those times we walked together along Shandling beach with the waves lapping peacefully against the rocks, the silence broken only by the occasional seagull gliding overhead. Words did not need to be spoken did they Wilf – our understanding of each other was stronger than ever. Remember those times. Please.

Time alone can be frightening when so much time has been spent together but you need to explore the world, explore your environment and find new companions with varied interests. Assure me Wilfred that you will take care of yourself. You are so special and will always be close to my heart, wherever that may be.

Wilfred I must go now, not because I want to but it waits like a carriage forcing me to get on, even though I have so much still to do.

Take care dearest. You are with me always.

Love,

Winifred

Figure 7.4 Imagining the contents of the letter left for Mr Wintergarten

Meeting Mr Wintergarten

Rose soon enters the house only to be told to 'clear off' by Mr Wintergarten. Once Rose has left the house the text tells us that 'Mr Wintergarten slowly pushed back his chair – and did something he hadn't done in years ...' Pause at this point and invite ideas from the children. Responses may include that he called her back, he went outside, he smiled or that he smelt the flowers.

Turn the page and read that Mr Wintergarten opened the curtains. At this point storytell the next part of the story. This will involve moving away from the actual text and imagining a new event in the text. You could say something like 'and as the sun streamed in and lit up the room for the first time, casting the shadows that had lurked there for years into hiding, Mr Wintergarten felt the warmth, the love and the compassion of his community. Turning away from the window, Mr Wintergarten went into his bedroom and knelt beside his bed. Reaching underneath he pulled out the large wooden chest which had been left and forgotten. He wiped away the dust, unlocked it with the rusting key and opened the chest. Reaching in he gently picked up the letter which he had not had the courage to read ... until now. Mr Wintergarten carefully opened the letter and, as a tear trickled down his cheek, he started to read the hand-written words'. In my experience at this point the class is still and listening to every word you say. You could ponder and question who the letter might be from. Maybe it is from his daughter and Rose reminds him of her, maybe from his son who has been out fighting for the army, possibly it is from his wife left for him at a pertinent time. ... Hand out paper for the children. They should first decide who the author of the letter would be and then imagine what its purpose was. If the story has captured children's interest and they feel a connection with the character your classroom should be abuzz with writing. It would be fantastic if you and any adults in the class could also write a letter at the same time as the children.

If you are working with younger children you may prefer to replace the letter with a picture. Mr Wintergarten reaches into his box and pulls out a picture or a photo which he has not had the courage to look at until now. Children could imagine what or who the picture would be of. You could also encourage children to think of what the message might be on the back of the picture.

Continue reading the story to the last double-page spread which shows a transformed community. Take time to compare this with the first double-page spread. Discuss what has changed both in the community as a whole and to the individuals. Move the discussion on to talking about the messages the book gives us.

Make this your own

There are many opportunities to expand the narrative within this drama. You may want to explore in more detail the life of Mr Wintergarten. We are not told a great deal about him in the story so there are many gaps to fill. You may also want to look at what the house and road would be like in a month's time, a year's time or 10 years' time. When I work with children around this text we take time looking at the final double-page spread and imagine that in 10 years' time when Mr Wintergarten dies a statue is erected in memory of him. Children form a group tableaux to represent what the story means to them.

*

ON SUDDEN HILL (2014, SIMON & SCHUSTER) BY LINDA SARAH AND BENJI DAVIES

- **Possible writing opportunities**: Making imaginary worlds
- **Interactive strategies**: Body percussion, role play, role on the wall, teacher in role (TiR)
- **Age range**: 3–7

Introduction

This is a story about friendship, change and growing up. We meet two characters, Birt and Etho, who are the closest of friends. They play together, laugh together and inhabit imaginary spaces together. Everything is perfect until Shu arrives. Shu had watched the boys play, seen their friendship and after plucking up the courage asked to join in. However Shu's inclusion changed the atmosphere causing Birt to feel different about the relationship and choose to stay at home. In the end the three resolve their differences, accept the change and forge a greater and stronger friendship than ever before. This is a perfect story for children who may be experiencing friendship issues. It also can support an understanding of family change when a new brother or sister is born or when a parent may meet a new partner.

Teaching objectives

- Develop willingness to accept and respect the ideas of others and to build on them.
- Identify with characters and actions through role-playing.
- Create and take part in improvised scenes.
- Gain confidence in their own abilities, particularly to communicate verbally and non-verbally.
- Contribute ideas through using the imagination.

Problems, emotions or challenges to be explore

- The main issue within this story concerns the feelings associated with true friendship and the sense of sadness when we come to realise that possibly our friend does not hold our friendship with the significance that we do.

The session

The ideas presented are intended to be adapted and shaped by you for use in your class. They are not intended as a formula to follow or as a lesson plan. You may feel that you would like, for example, to take one idea and expand on it depending on the interests of your class or you may want to sequence a few of the ideas together. The text should help inspire teaching with a purpose which creates passion and empowers the class. This will depend, not only on the interests of your class, but also on your characteristics as a teacher. Some ideas will resonate more strongly with you than others. I hope the ideas you do use and embellish will mean that your class encounters imaginative teaching with purpose and passion for empowerment.

Connecting with the theme

Discuss with the children the concept of friendship. Explore the attributes and characteristics of a good friend. You could use the role on the wall convention to build up a pictorial account of the characteristics of a friend. You could link this to other stories you have read together. Can children think of examples of characters who have these attributes? Ask the children to describe the activities they enjoy doing with their friends.

Introducing the text

Explain that the book we are going to share is, among other things, about friendship. Ask children to predict what they expect from the illustration on the front cover. Show the children the front cover. Does it complement their expectations? Take time to look at the illustration and identify the two characters, how they are feeling and the location where the story takes place. Also show the double-page title page where the two boys are climbing over the fence to head up to Sudden Hill. Ask the children why they think the boys have cardboard boxes with them.

Read the first two pages. Ask the children for what they would use the boxes for? What games and imaginative experiences would they develop? Aim to obtain a variety of large boxes which you could put in one of the areas in the classroom in order for the children to experiment with their own ideas. Throughout the school day you may see the boxes used for a variety of purposes. Some children may turn them into cars, fire engines, boats, fortresses or castles whereas others may make the boxes into a den, a classroom or may enjoy curling up with a book or magazine.

The tune of the text

Continue reading to the point where it says 'Birt loves their two-by-two rhythm'. Discuss with the children what this might mean. Can anyone use body percussion to show what this might sound like? Invite the children to march around the room in a two-by-two rhythm. Gather a range of percussion instruments and invite children to experiment playing a two-by-two rhythm. Groups could take it in turn to play their rhythm while the other children march around the room. Discuss how this relates to friendship and ask the children for examples of times when they have been in a two-by-two rhythm. This could be for example when they are walking with their friend.

Read to the point where Shu is at the bottom of Sudden Hill with his box. Look at the picture and ask the children what they think Birt and Etho might be thinking. Role play this scene with you taking the role of Shu asking if you can join in their game. Invite the children to decide if they will be Birt or Etho and then to respond to your question asking if you can join in their game.

Feeling left out

Look at the next picture and, after discussing the scene, focus on Birt. What do the children notice about him? How do they think he might be feeling? Why might he be feeling like this? Have the children in the class ever felt left out?

Use the role on the wall technique to generate words to describe how Birt is feeling. Talk to the children about what Etho and Shu could do to make Birt feel better. What would the class children do in this situation? Role play the scene in the class with one child taking the role of Birt and other children taking the role of Etho or Shu.

Tell the children that although the suggestions did make Birt feel a bit better at first he still felt left out when he saw Etho and Shu playing as it reminded him of the special bond he used to have with Etho. Read the next few pages to the point where Etho and Shu knock on Birt's door. Role play the conversation which might take place building on the ideas shared previously.

Read to the end of the story where all three boys are now friends. Talk to the children about what they could do if they see someone on the playground without a friend to play with. Does the story help them understand their feelings better?

Make this your own

The theme of this story about making and accepting friends will resonate with every teacher. You could extend this by using some of the texts within the literature links section to look at other aspects of friendship. For example the excellent text *Oliver* by Birgitta Sif introduces us to a boy who does not seem to have many friends and sees everyone as different from himself. Oliver therefore spends a lot of time in his own imagination sometimes distancing himself from others. It is only when he finally meets a girl who he can relate to and who likes the same things as him that he is able have someone to share in his games and imaginary world.

*

LITERATURE LINKS RELATING TO THE THEME

There are many other books which explore the theme of this chapter. You may want to use them to complement the work you are doing or see how some of the drama strategies will enable you to enrich the learning experience. Suitable recommendations for use with process drama include:

Fox (2008, Allen & Unwin) by Margaret Wild and Ron Brooks

My Dad (2003, Doubleday Childrens) by Anthony Browne

My Mum (2008, Doubleday Childrens) by Anthony Browne

A Bad Case of Stripes (2000, Scholastic) by David Shannon

Scaredy Squirrel Makes a Friend (2008, Catnip) by Melanie Watt

Bluebird (2014, Anderson Press) by Bob Staake

Denver (2012, Anderson Press) by David McKee.

8 Creative ideas with texts
Rhyme and rhythm

Before writing was invented, memory was crucial in order to share information. In oral cultures stories were used to remind, warn, teach and inform communities and future generations. Often the stories would have patterns to them in order for them to be remembered. Rhyme and rhythm therefore featured strongly and are part of our ancestry. Indeed it was Socrates who warned of the dangers of the invention of writing saying that it would produce forgetfulness in the minds of those who used it. We may be able to relate to this in our own work-feeling the need to refer to notes and jottings to aid our memory. This section focuses on how the rhythm and rhyme of a text can actually move us in a way which enables us to feel the text within us. This feeling in turn helps us to remember and internalise the words we are using.

THE RASCALLY CAKE (2009, ANDERSEN PRESS) BY JEANNE WILLIS AND KORKY PAUL

- **Possible writing opportunities**: Poetry, recipes
- **Interactive strategies**: Improvisation, role play
- **Age range**: 3–11

Introduction

I have a collection of books illustrated by Korky Paul and *The Rascally Cake* is certainly one of my favourites. This is an enjoyable story of a cake which comes to life and chases the creator of the cake, Mr Rufus Skumskins O'Parsley, around his house before fleeing. The book includes a range of disgusting ingredients which hopefully would never find their way near a cake but are extremely fun to imagine and play around with. The rhythm and rhyme of the text, the excellent pictures and the thought of the horrendous ingredients keep the reader captivated throughout.

Teaching objectives

- Understand and take pleasure in the difference between pretence and reality.
- Identify with characters and actions through role-playing.

- Create and take part in improvised scenes.
- Gain confidence in their own abilities, particularly to communicate verbally and non-verbally.
- Contribute ideas through using the imagination.

Problems, emotions or challenges to be explored

- The playful nature of this text draws the reader in as we join in and tune in with the rhyme and rhythm. There is a mischievous element to the text as we conjure up the most revolting recipe we can think of.
- The challenge is to create a recipe which is as disgusting as we can make it within the confines of classroom acceptability!

The session

The ideas presented are intended to be adapted and shaped by you for use in your class. They are not intended as a formula to follow or as a lesson plan. You may feel that you would like, for example, to take one idea and expand on it depending on the interests of your class or you may want to sequence a few of the ideas together. The text should help inspire teaching with a purpose which creates passion and empowers the class. This will depend, not only on the interests of your class, but also on your characteristics as a teacher. Some ideas will resonate more strongly with you than others. I hope the ideas you do use and embellish will mean that your class encounters imaginative teaching with purpose and passion for empowerment.

Connecting with the theme

Discuss with the class whether any of them enjoy baking or possibly watching some of the cooking shows shown on television. Take a straw poll of the types of baking the class has experience of. Then ask them to imagine their favourite meal. What does it look like, taste like and smell like. Hopefully the class will be salivating at the thought of some delicious meals! Then explain that the book is about a disgusting and indeed rascally cake.

  After exploring the front cover and introducing the children to both the author and the illustrator read (or if possible learn and recite) the first page while showing the illustration of Mr O'Parsley sat at his dining room table. Give time for the class to explore the illustrations in this text as on each reading there will be more to discover.

Imagining the ingredients

Read on to the point where it says,

> He smiled and smacked his lips with greed
> And scribbled down the things he'd need.

Cover the rest of the text and invite the children to talk in pairs about what ingredients they think he might write down. After a short period of time stop the class and ask for some ideas. Note the ideas on the flipchart and then model how you can embellish some of the ideas to make them even more disgusting! (Within reason!) For example one offering might be 'a fish eye' and you might embellish it by saying 'the stench from an oozing fish eye'. After modelling some examples give the children time to talk again before handing out sticky notes and inviting children, in pairs to write one idea for an ingredient on each sticky note. Then ask the children to form groups of four. They should share their ideas and come up with the best ten ingredients which they think are suitable and will interest the reader.

Uncover the ingredients shown in the text and continue to read and explore the pictures. Read the page which starts 'Two days later he came back'.

Feeling the rhyme and rhythm

There is a wonderful rhythm to this page where we can possibly picture Rufus gleefully moving around the cooking pot adding his ingredients. Concentrate on the following lines:

> In went a tramp's sock! In went the fleas!
> In went the scabs from a schoolboy's knees!
> In went a cowpat! In went mud!
> In went blubber, the bones and the blood!

Read these lines a few times encouraging children to join in with a range of body percussion. Children may, at first be comfortable with clicking their fingers to the beat as you read, then possibly tapping their tables before choosing an imaginary instrument to play along to the beat. Drums, triangles, cymbals and trumpets work especially well! The idea is for the children to feel the beat of the narrative within them. They may want to move in time to the beat or even dance. Then ask some children to join you in reciting the words while others play the instruments until all the children have heard and felt the tune of the text.

Creating the ingredients

Then remind the children about their own ideas for ingredients and challenge them, in groups, to come up with their own poem describing what went into the cake. Give children the freedom to explore and experiment with the language. Although you could count the syllables and identify the rhythmic pattern you will probably find that the earlier work has implicitly embedded the pattern with the children. Using their ideas on the sticky notes form the previous activity encourages the children to move their ideas around until they have a poem which they are happy with.

The performance of the poems can work in a number of ways. I have found that some groups add actions and movements to their performance so sometimes need 'preparation' time. Therefore I often ask the whole class to read:

Two days later he came back
And grinning like a maniac,
Put on his apron and his hat
And heated up the cooking fat.

The class read this in-between each group's performance. This gives the group about to perform some time to get themselves ready and also gives the cue to start.

Read the rest of the story encouraging children to join in and also explore the illustrations. The final picture of a supposedly reformed Rufus sat at his dining room table offers a stark contrast to the first picture explored. However careful examination may reveal that not everything has changed!

Make this your own

There are great opportunities to continue playing with language either with this text or others listed in the literature links at the end of this chapter. *The Rascally Cake* offers opportunities for looking at recipes. Maybe you could use it at the start of the year for children to write 'what makes me' recipes. To do this you should think about a range of human qualities such as humour, compassion, work ethic and perseverance. Make a long list and then children can think about which qualities best describe them and which are more prevalent. Using traditional recipes as a scaffold, children can then use these features to construct their recipe with lines such as 'a pinch of humour guaranteed to brighten up any day'. The recipes could be put into a class book for everyone to share at the start of the year.

*

CLICK, CLACK, MOO COWS THAT TYPE (2010, LITTLE SIMON) BY DOREEN CRONIN ILLUSTRATED BY BETSY LEWIN

* **Possible writing opportunities**: Note and letter writing, persuasive writing

* **Interactive strategies**: teacher in role (TiR)

* **Age range**: 3–7

Introduction

Farmer Brown has a problem. Believe it or not his cows like to type and send a range of demands to the farmer. Not content with their own demands the cows soon get the hens on side and threaten to go on strike if their demands are not met. As the demands grow, Farmer Brown gets more frustrated until he types his own note back to the cows and hens. This leads to a meeting where a compromise is reached with the farmer giving in to the demands if the typewriter is forfeited.

Teaching objectives

- Develop willingness to accept and respect the ideas of others and to build on them.
- Contribute ideas through using the imagination.
- Identify with characters and actions through role-playing
- Learn how to work together to solve human and practical problems.
- Gain confidence in their own abilities, particularly to communicate verbally and non-verbally.
- Understand and take pleasure in the difference between pretence and reality.

Problems, emotions or challenges to be explored

- The main problem encountered in this story is the difference of opinion between the farmer (the employer) and the animals (the workers). The animals feel they should be entitled to better conditions but the farmer is reluctant to oblige!
- The challenge for the farmer is how to ensure his farm can continue to operate without him giving in to all the demands of the animals.

The session

The ideas presented are intended to be adapted and shaped by you for use in your class. They are not intended as a formula to follow or as a lesson plan. You may feel that you would like, for example, to take one idea and expand on it depending on the interests of your class or you may want to sequence a few of the ideas together. The text should help inspire teaching with a purpose which creates passion and empowers the class. This will depend, not only on the interests of your class, but also on your characteristics as a teacher. Some ideas will resonate more strongly with you than others. I hope the ideas you do use and embellish will mean that your class encounters imaginative teaching with purpose and passion for empowerment.

Introducing the text

Introduce the book by discussing other texts children know about which involve farms or animals. Make a list and identify similarities and differences between them. Look at whether the animals featured in the stories take on any human characteristics. Discuss the effect this has on the reader. Show the front cover and make predictions based on the illustration and the title.

Read the first page where we are told that all day long Farmer Brown hears:

> Click, clack, moo.
> Click, clack, moo.
> Clickety, clack, moo.

Read it once to the class and then invite them to join in telling them that this appears a few times throughout the text and you would like the class to recite it with you each time.

Playful imaginings

Read on a couple of pages to the point where we are told that the cows left a new note on the barn door. We have already discovered that the cows have demanded electric blankets so ponder with the class what other demands they might have. Children will enjoy thinking about a range of possibilities including regular pizza deliveries, a massage, a holiday in the sun and many more! Hand out sticky notes and ask the children to write their note and then come and stick it on the classroom door. Enjoy sharing some of the ides the children have thought of.

Display the next page which shows the note the cows left on the barn door. The class will notice the dramatic silhouette of the farmer. This is a great opportunity to explore how the farmer feels after reading the note. Ask the class how they know what the farmer is feeling as there aren't any words to communicate this to us. Talk to the class about the importance of reading the illustrations. You may want to develop this idea by working with the children to recreate a range of other silhouettes to depict other emotions.

The rumblings and grumblings of the farmer

Read on to the point where the farmer received another note, this time explaining that the hens are also cold and would like electric blankets! Tell the class that the farmer was extremely upset and after reading the note was stomping around the farm mumbling under his breath. As teacher in role act out what the farmer may have been doing as you walk around the classroom mumbling and possibly stomping your feet. Invite the children to join you as the farmer walking around the classroom. Ensure you model quiet mumbling so that all children can hear you as you tell them that every so often some of the mumbling became audible and was an indicator of the disgruntlement the farmer felt at this time.

Explain that you are going to move among the children and when you tap them on the shoulder they should make their mumbling audible and speak out the farmer's thoughts at this time. Children may say, for example, 'I just won't let this continue, they have gone too far this time', or, 'They have tried my patience to the limit – just wait until tomorrow when they will regret this'.

An angry response

Continue reading to the point where we are told that 'Farmer Brown was furious.' Storytell how the farmer was so furious that he went into his own house, got out his own typewriter and typed his own letter to the cows and hens! Explore with the children what this might have said before giving them the opportunity to write (or type) the letter they imagine the farmer would have sent.

Read the letter in the text which the farmer typed and compare it with those thought of by the class. You will often find that the ideas from the class will show clearly the displeasure the farmer is feeling. Read on to the point where the cows hold an emergency meeting to decide how they should respond to the farmer's demands. You could recreate the meeting in small groups. Tell the children that the meeting was going well until the idea which came from one of the cows was so daring it startled the rest of the group. Invite the children in groups to think about what this suggestion could have been. Tell them to create the freeze-frame of the moment the suggestion was posed. After giving time for the groups to think about what could have been suggested count down from five to zero when the groups should freeze. Storytell the narrative of the meeting and interweave the suggestions from the groups into the narrative.

Continue reading the text to the point where the ducks send their note to the farmer. Ask the children what you think the farmer's response would be before showing them the final illustration. It seems as if the animals might be taking over the farm.

Make this your own

You could extend the drama by imagining what might take place in the future at the farm. Ask the children to imagine what the farm might be like in a week's time or even a month's time. You could tell the children that Mrs Brown, the farmer's wife, has been away on holiday and is due to return very soon. When she does return, steps out of the taxi and makes her way down the path to the farm what does she notice first of all? As she gets closer what other things does she notice and then as she enters the farm house what does she see?

*

LITERATURE LINKS RELATING TO THE THEME

There are many other books which explore the theme of this chapter. You may want to use them to complement the work you are doing or see how some of the drama strategies will enable you to enrich the learning experience. Suitable recommendations for use with process drama include:

Snail's Legs (2006, Frances Lincoln) by Damian Harvey and Korky Paul

The Wonkey Donkey (1999, Red Fox) by Jonathan Long and Korky Paul

Dodo Doo-Doo (2011, Hodder Children's books) by Kaye Umansky and Korky Paul

Tiny Little Fly (2010, Walker books) by Michael Rosen and Kevin Waldron

Walking Through the Jungle (1993, Walker books) by Julie Lacome

Tanka Tanka Stunk! (2003, Red Fox) by Steve Webb

Down by the Cool of the Pool (2000, Orchard books) by Tony Mitton and Guy Parker-Rees

The Scarecrows' Wedding (2014, Alison Green Books) by Julia Donaldson and Axel Scheffer

A Squash and a Squeeze (2003, Macmillan Children's Books) by Julia Donaldson and Axel Scheffler.

9 Creative ideas with texts
War and conflict

With the increased exposure to the news via interactive devices, there can be no doubt that children are coming into contact with stories and images about events in our world at an earlier age and possibly on a more regular basis. In my class we used to watch the BBC programme *Newsround* in order to comment on world events and share differing perceptions. This was always an interesting time as we were able to talk about where our views and values come from and how our perceptions are shaped. In addition to watching and commenting on the news we would also use a range of texts in order to experience the situation others may be in and be able to look at differing perspectives.

THE SILENCE SEEKER (2009, TAMARIND) BY BEN MORLEY, ILLUSTRATED BY CARL PEARCE

- **Possible writing opportunities**: Creating maps, writing in role
- **Interactive strategies**: Role on the wall, forum theatre, thought tracking, freeze-frame, hot seating
- **Age range**: 5–11

Introduction

Ben Morley is a well-travelled writer who currently lives in Singapore but has also worked in Poland, Borneo, China and London. His first book *The Silence Seeker* introduces us to a family who have just had some new neighbours move in. Joe's mum explains that the new family are asylum seekers who are looking for peace and quiet. Joe mishears his mum and thinks that they are silence seekers and therefore is curious as to why they have come to such a busy city in search of silence. Joe takes it upon himself to help the boy who has moved with his family to search for silence. In their search a friendship develops between the two boys but Joe soon realises what a noisy city it is.

Teaching objectives

- Develop willingness to accept and respect the ideas of others and to build on them.
- Identify with characters and actions through role-playing.
- Have the confidence and ability to put across a particular point of view.

- Use questioning to seek out further information.
- Learn how to work together to solve human and practical problems.
- Create and take part in improvised scenes in order to explore particular issues which could, for instance, have a practical, social or moral dimension.
- Gain confidence in their own abilities, particularly to communicate verbally and non-verbally.
- Contribute ideas through using the imagination.
- Realise that the views of individuals do not always coincide.

Problems, emotions or challenges to be explored

- The first issue concerns the concept of asylum seekers and children's understanding of the term. They may already have developed views about asylum seekers due to events in the news.
- The second issue is about friendship and caring for one another. Joe extends his hand of friendship to someone he does not know. This raises moral issues for us to consider whether we would be so accommodating.

The session

The ideas presented are intended to be adapted and shaped by you for use in your class. They are not intended as a formula to follow or as a lesson plan. You may feel that you would like, for example, to take one idea and expand on it depending on the interests of your class or you may want to sequence a few of the ideas together. The text should help inspire teaching with a purpose which creates passion and empowers the class. This will depend, not only on the interests of your class, but also on your characteristics as a teacher. Some ideas will resonate more strongly with you than others. I hope the ideas you do use and embellish will mean that your class encounters imaginative teaching with purpose and passion for empowerment.

Connecting with the theme

To introduce the theme show the children a shoe box. Within it put five items or objects which are important to you. Explain to the children that this is your special box wherein you have put possessions which you would not want to be without. They are special and particular to you. You could ask the children to predict what type of objects might be in the box. Open the box and talk the children through the items. Discuss how these are not items such as a television or a multimedia device but instead items which are personal and relate directly to your life.

Invite the children to consider what they would have in their box. Give them the opportunity to discuss their items in small groups. Ask questions to encourage children to give reasons for their choices. You may want children to draw the items and put them into a box. Decorating the outside would also indicate things, people, events and places which are important to them.

Alternatively you could ask, with parents' permission, for children to bring in a special item from home. The item should be important to them. Children may choose, among other things, to bring in a photo, a book, a bracelet, a toy or an ornament. Time needs to be given for children to talk about their objects. In effect the children will be creating a story around their object, explaining why it is important, what the significance is, the event or events in their lives where it has been most pertinent and where it is kept at home. Organise a carousel of storytelling so children can refine their stories. This could be achieved through asking children to think about a title for their story or event and displaying it in order to entice people to hear it. Alternatively you could set up a storytelling ring doughnut. In order to do this you form two circles of chairs facing each other. These will be the inner ring and the outer ring.

Introduce the theme using a range of newspaper articles and news clips to raise the issue of asylum seekers. Discuss with the children what their understanding of asylum seekers is. There are many sources of information to ensure factual information is used within discussions. You may like to look at information from the Red Cross or the Refugee Council. Using a large map of the world would enable children to be able to identify the countries from which people are seeking asylum.

Introducing the text

Show the front cover of the text 'The Silence Seeker'. Explain that the story is about a boy who moves into a new neighbourhood and makes friends with his neighbour Joe. Give time to children to look at the cover. Lead the discussion focusing on why the text is called 'The Silence Seeker' rather than 'The Asylum Seeker'. Focus on the two boys sat on the doorstep. Which do they think is Joe and which is the asylum seeker? The discussion may raise issues regarding assumptions made about asylum seekers. Notice the different expressions on the faces of the boys as well as their body language.

Prepare two outlines on large paper. One will represent Joe and the other will represent the asylum seeker. Explain that we will add thoughts, feelings and actions to the outlines throughout the text as we learn more about the characters. To start with ask the children what different thoughts may be going through the boys' minds. Children could discuss and then note ideas on individual thought bubbles before sharing with the whole class. Aim to capture these thoughts and represent them as thought bubbles on the outlines.

Discussing possibilities

Read the text to the point where we are told that the boy sits on the doorstep every day and sometimes closes his eyes. Referring to the information gathered before starting the text pose some questions to the children such as: What might he be thinking about? Where might he have come from? What can he remember about his homeland? Add the children's suggestions to the outline created earlier.

Continue the story and explore the character of Joe. We find out that he makes two sandwiches and wants to help his new friend find the silence that he craves. Start to add some thoughts about Joe's character to the outline. Children may consider words such as trusting, helpful, friendly, compassionate and selfless. Discussions may also consider the naivety of Joe as well as possibly questioning the nature of the decision leading to him exploring a city with someone he does not know. Relate this situation to the children's own lives and consider whether they would take the same action.

Searching for silence

Return to the text and read the pages which tell us of all the different places Joe takes his friend in search of silence. In Joe's day-to-day life it could be assumed that he thought these were quiet places and as such had tuned out some of the inherent noise that he only now notices because he is searching for silence. On each page we see the boys standing together. Choose one of the scenes such as the double page depicting the canal scene. Explain that we will be exploring the interior thoughts of the boys as they look down over the canal. This could be done as a whole class as described here or alternatively could take place in smaller groups. Set up the scene in the classroom. Ask the children to form a circle as if they are on the edge of the story looking in at the events. Within the circle describe the setting for the class so they can get a feeling for where the canal is and the position of the bridge where the boys are standing. Choose two children to take the role of the boys. Invite help from the class to decide on how they would be standing, their body language and their facial expression. Storytell the events leading up to the point where the boys are looking down at the canal. Joe, in his heart, hopes he has at last found the silence he thinks his friend is searching for but looking down he heard just how noisy the area is. Freeze the scene and invite children to explore what the interior thoughts of the boys might be. This can be achieved in a number of ways but you may want to invite the children forming the circle to be ready to voice what one of the boys might be thinking. When they are ready they should step on to the freeze-frame, touch one of the boys on the shoulder and speak their thoughts before returning to the circle.

Stop to consider the school environment. Are there any places within the school environment which are havens of silence? Give the children a map of the school and ask them to identify areas of quiet. Children could devise a key to accompany their map. You may also want children to consider how the noise in these places may change depending on the time of day.

Generating questions from the text

Read to the end of the text. Revisit the outlines representing Joe and the asylum seeker. Explain that the text leaves us with lots of questions. Invite the children to note their questions on sticky notes ready to stick on to the outlines. This will involve them asking questions as a reader but you may also want them to ask questions in role. For example, what questions would Joe have which he would like to ask his friend who has gone? You could possibly hot seat Joe to find out how he is feeling about his friend disappearing.

Consider where Joe's friend has gone. Discuss with the children the range of possibilities. If possible use a real-life example of the journey of an asylum seeker. Explore the reasons for the need to move house at such short notice. Decide as a class where you think he may be now. Then imagine that the asylum seeker is sat on another doorstep in another place. Invite children to go into role as the asylum seeker and consider what thoughts and feelings might be going through his mind. Thought track the thoughts by moving around the class and indicating which children should voice their ideas, in role, as the asylum seeker.

Make this your own

The children have generated a range of ideas throughout the session and will have developed their understanding of asylum seekers, relationships, friendships and separation. You may want to explore how the children might express these in a written form. Therefore you could ask children to imagine that they are either Joe or the asylum seeker sitting on the doorstep wherever they may be. They reach into their pocket and pull out a piece of paper. Not knowing what it is or where it came from, they open it to realise that it is a letter or note from their friend. Joe reads the letter from his friend the asylum seeker and the asylum seeker reads the letter from Joe. What might it say? Drawing on information gathered through the sessions and also using the text children could write the letter from the perspective of one of the characters.

*

BLODIN THE BEAST (1996, FRANCES LINCOLN CHILDREN'S BOOKS) BY MICHAEL MORPURGO

- **Possible writing opportunities**: Diary entries

- **Interactive strategies**: Storytelling in role, freeze-frame, drawing, improvisation, role play, group sculpture

- **Age range**: 6–11

Introduction

This brilliant book by the acclaimed author Michael Morpurgo with illustrations by Christina Balit tells the story of a beast who stalks the land terrorising the inhabitants. As the beast destroyed each village he enslaved the people forcing them to dig for oil. In the last village lived an old man, Shanga, who refused to flee in the wake of the beast, deciding instead to stay and finish his weaving. Hosea, a young boy with no family of his own, decided to stay with Shanga until the beast arrived. When finally it was too dangerous to stay Shanga gave the carpet he had been weaving to Hosea. This has particular significance and is used to guide Hosea to safety and the eventual destruction of the beast.

Teaching objectives

- Use questioning to seek out further information.
- Contribute ideas through using the imagination.
- Gain confidence in their own abilities, particularly to communicate verbally and non-verbally.
- Explore the variety of human emotions.
- Use a range of dramatic forms to express ideas and feelings.
- Understand and take pleasure in the difference between pretence and reality.

Problems, emotions or challenges to be explored

- The first problem concerns the feeling of fear as the beast makes its way towards the village. There is palpable concern that the whole village will be destroyed and the inhabitants enslaved.
- The emotional challenge is about the need to leave someone we love and respect, knowing that they will meet their fate, in order to save the village.
- The main problem is one of David and Goliath where the beast seems all-powerful and destructive and Shangra, the boy, only has wisdom on his side.

The session

The ideas presented are intended to be adapted and shaped by you for use in your class. They are not intended as a formula to follow or as a progressive lesson plan. You may feel that you would like, for example, to take one idea and expand on it depending on the interests of your class or you may want to sequence a few of the ideas together. The text should create teaching with a purpose which creates passion and empowerment for the class. This will depend on not only the interests of your class but also on your characteristics as a teacher. Some ideas will resonate more strongly with you than others. I hope the ideas you do use and embellish will mean that your class encounters teaching with purpose and passion for empowerment.

Introducing the text

Show the front cover of the text to the class and facilitate a discussion about what they notice, the links they can make and their predictions for the story. Children may have read other texts by Michael Morpurgo so could draw on prior knowledge of his style of writing.

Turn to the inside cover which shows two of the characters in the story. Allow children to make predictions about their involvement in the story. Again work with the class to analyse where their assumptions are coming from. What links to other texts are they making?

Generating stories to share

Read the opening page which tells us about the destructive nature of the beast and the fear he puts into the villagers. At the end of the page storytell how a group of villagers, after hearing the beast approaching, fled up the mountain to, what they hoped would be, an area of safety. There they met with other villagers, some who had escaped from the slavery, others who, like themselves, had fled from their ruined village. Explain that as they all mingled they shared stories about the beast. Some stories were true, some were retold and some were from their darkest imagining. Invite the children, in pairs, to make up a story to be retold. Then ask the children to form groups of four to practice telling their stories to each other.

Tell the class that as darkness drew in the villagers came together, formed a circle and started to share their stories. Start off by telling your own story, modelling the tone and style associated with the storytelling as the sun goes down. Give enough time for the children who also want to share their tales of the beast to do so.

Dreams of the beast

After the stories are told explain that the villagers were getting tired. They arranged for each of the villagers to take turns in keeping a look out throughout the night while the rest slept. However as they drifted off their sleep was overtaken by thoughts about what their village would be like now with their friends enslaved and Blodin the beast watching over them, terrifying them. Invite the children, in groups, to produce a freeze-frame of their depiction of the scene. Before counting down to freeze the scenes ask the children to think of a caption which depicts their freeze-frame.

Read the next page which tells us that Blodin is getting closer. The villagers panic but Shanga, the oldest and wisest man, refuses to go. As the teacher, go into role as Shanga explaining why you will stay in the village and wait for Blodin. Ask the children (the villagers) to come close as you give them the wisdom of your years and then invite them to ask any questions they may have. Answer the questions in role as Shanga. Make reference to the importance of the carpet you are weaving in your responses.

Saying goodbye

Read the first paragraph of the third page. Tell the villagers they must get ready to go but you will be waiting in the mouth of your cave as they leave the village in small groups. Give the children time to think about what their last words to Shanga might be, before organising them to leave the village.

Read to the end of the page where Hosea is told by Shanga about the significance of the carpet. Discuss the line 'there is more than wool in this carpet.' Ask the children what they think Shanga may mean by this. Some children may think the carpet contains characteristics or attributes such as bravery, strength or faith needed to defeat the beast. Other children may feel that the carpet contains pictures or clues. Hand out small pieces of paper, maybe A5, and ask

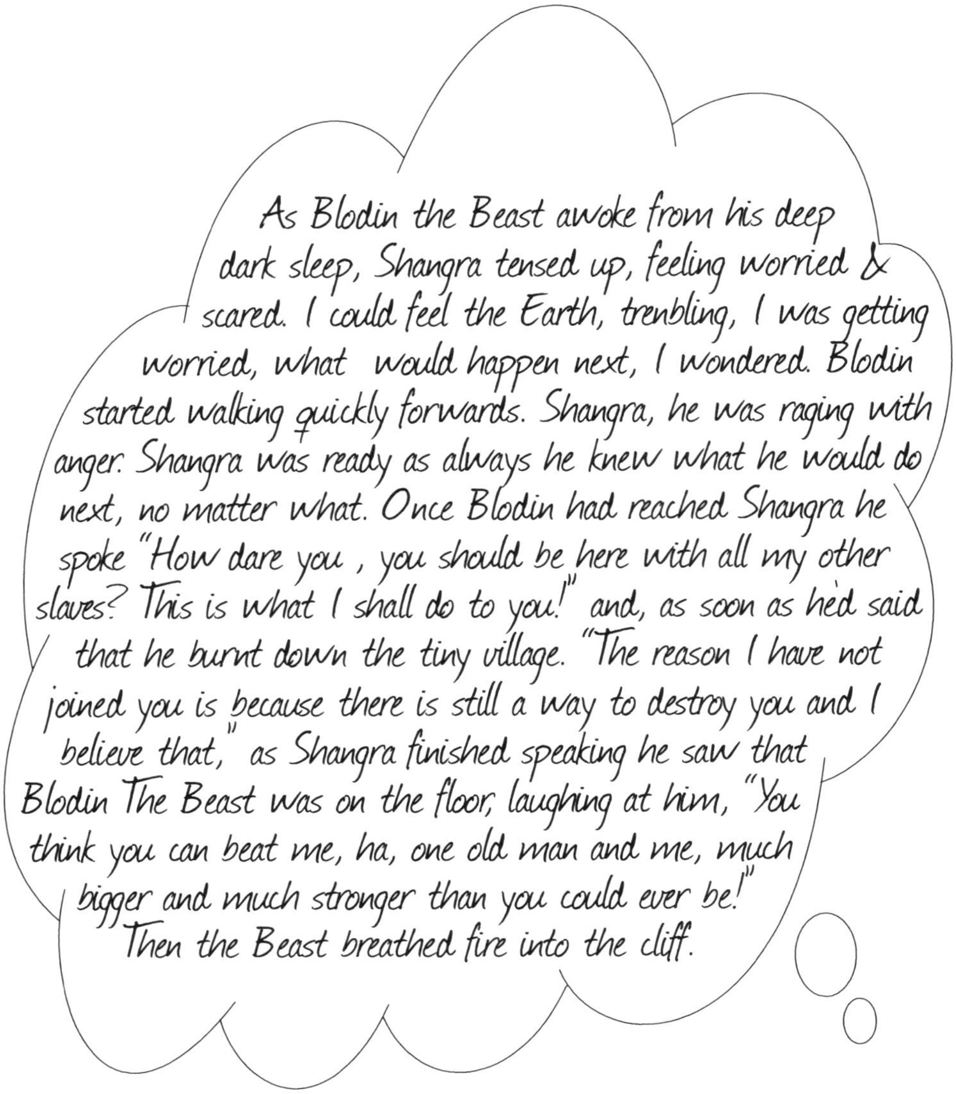

> As Blodin the Beast awoke from his deep dark sleep, Shangra tensed up, feeling worried & scared. I could feel the Earth, trembling, I was getting worried, what would happen next, I wondered. Blodin started walking quickly forwards. Shangra, he was raging with anger. Shangra was ready as always he knew what he would do next, no matter what. Once Blodin had reached Shangra he spoke "How dare you , you should be here with all my other slaves? This is what I shall do to you!" and, as soon as he'd said that he burnt down the tiny village. "The reason I have not joined you is because there is still a way to destroy you and I believe that," as Shangra finished speaking he saw that Blodin The Beast was on the floor, laughing at him, "You think you can beat me, ha, one old man and me, much bigger and much stronger than you could ever be!" Then the Beast breathed fire into the cliff.

Figure 9.1 Dreaming about the meeting between Shanga and Blodin the Beast

the children to write or draw what they think their piece of carpet may contain. These can then be put together to form the large carpet. Give time for the children to explore the carpet, looking at other children's thoughts and ideas.

Read the next two pages where Shanga tells Hosea to take the carpet and go. Tell the children that as he goes he starts to imagine one of the events he thinks he will experience. Children might draw on what Shanga has told them or they may elaborate on part of the class carpet they have constructed. In small groups invite the children to improvise a scene from one of Hosea's imagined events. Tell the children that their improvisation should be no longer than 20 seconds and it should be clear for others to understand the event they are describing. After some thinking and practice time, invite the groups to show their improvisations while you narrate between them.

The wise words of Shanga

Read on to the point where Hosea has gone through the desert and found an area to rest and eventually sleep. As he slept he dreamt of Shanga and his probable encounter with Blodin. Display the double-page picture to the children with the writing removed and recreate the scene in the classroom by dividing the class into two. Half will represent Blodin and the other half will represent Shanga. Invite the respective sides to consider what they might say to each other. Narrate some examples for the children which they may want to use and expand on in their own ideas.

Structure the improvisation to ensure that all voices can be heard by possibly storytelling the lead into the dream telling how Shanga sat at the mouth of his cave showing no fear or anxiety as the beast, full of destruction, came closer and closer. Then, in role as Shanga, join the group and support the development of the argument teasing out the reason for Blodin to be destroying the villages. Seek to find out why Blodin has come to this area, where he was before, what his intentions are and whether he feels any sorrow for what he is doing. Blodin will be seeking to discover why Shanga has not shown fear like everyone else, why he has stayed, why he will not submit and save himself and why is he not scared of death?

Read the text from page 8 which tells of the dream and of Shanga's death. Draw the class together and discuss the points raised from the debate and the dream.

Concluding the drama

Continue reading to the end of the story. Discuss with the children the themes which have emerged from the work they have done. In essence the text is about the force of good and evil, how faith, determination and self-belief can overcome even the mightiest barriers and how life experience can give an enhanced perspective on situations. Invite the children, in small groups, to consider the themes and then to create a group sculpture summarising the theme which is most pertinent to them. While working on their sculpture ask the groups to also think of a title for their group sculpture.

Look at the sculptures one at a time and record the titles on the flipchart. Once all the sculptures have been seen discuss any similarities between the titles. Invite children to draw comparisons with other stories they know.

Make this your own

You could imagine that Shangra had left a final letter for Hosea which is only found when he returns to the village. Nestled just within the cave entrance there is a rock with paper underneath. Hosea takes it and reads Shangra's final words for him. Imagine with the children what the letter would say. What wise words would Shangra use and what wisdom would he impart?

*

LITERATURE LINKS RELATING TO THE THEME

There are many other books which explore the theme of this chapter. You may want to use them to complement the work you are doing or see how some of the drama strategies will enable you to enrich the learning experience. Suitable recommendations for use with process drama include:

Good Night, Commander (2010, Groundwood Books) by Ahmad Akbarpour

Playing War (2005, Tilbury House Publishers) by Kathy Beckwith

The Enemy: A Book About Peace (2009, Schwartz & Wade Books) by Davide Cali and Serge Bloch

The Sky of Afghanistan (2012, Cuento de Luz SL) by Ana A de Eulate

A Child's Garden: A Story of Hope (2010, Walker books) by Michael Foreman

The Conquerors (2005, Anderson Press) by David McKee

The Peace Book (2009, Little Brown US) by Todd Parr

Silent Music: A Story of Baghdad (2008, Roaring Brook Press) by James Rumford

The War (2007, First Avenue Editions) by Anais Vaugelade

The Butter Battle Book (1984, Random House Books) by Dr. Seuss.

10 Creative ideas with texts
Nature

The themes of nature, recycling and sustainability pervade the primary curriculum often forming part of Geography, History or PSHE. We encourage our children to appreciate their surroundings and to take care of it. Some schools have environmental clubs, forest schools, allotments and work on a sustainability model. In whatever way we are able, from growing beans in the classroom to experiencing a school farm we are developing the idea of the need to protect, preserve and care for our environment. Often the classroom rules will reflect this as well, helping children understand about the importance of not wasting classroom resources. The texts identified in this section can complement the work within the class by focusing on the power of nature and also the need to look at our environment and value what may be seen as the smallest of things.

THE PAPERBAG PRINCE (1994, RED FOX) BY COLIN THOMSON

- **Possible writing opportunities**: Campaigning posters, letter writing, diary entry
- **Interactive strategies**: Freeze-frame, role play, improvisation, forum theatre, thought tracking
- **Age range**: 5–11

Introduction

If you have not come across the author/illustrator Colin Thomson I would encourage you to have a look at his work. This book, *The Paperbag Prince*, like so many of his other titles is superbly illustrated which encourages the reader to pore over the illustrations time and time again spotting elements not seen before and making links between different illustrations as the book is read. The story centres around the Paperbag Prince who lives on a rubbish dump in an old railway carriage. Since his farmhouse burnt down and the council gave the land over for a rubbish dump, the Paperbag Prince had cycled each day to the dump, content to be amid nature. It is a story of the power of nature, the importance of appreciating personal stories and for me it resonates with the importance of taking time out of a busy world to sit, relax and reflect.

Teaching objectives

- Identify with characters and actions through role playing.
- Have the confidence and ability to put across a particular point of view.

- Realise that the views of individuals do not always coincide.

- Contribute ideas through using the imagination.

- Use a range of dramatic forms to express ideas and feelings.

- Gain confidence in their own abilities, particularly to communicate verbally and non-verbally.

- Create and take part in improvised scenes in order to explore particular issues which could, for instance, have a practical, social or moral dimension.

Problems, emotions or challenges to be explored

- The main problem tackled in this drama is the conflict between the desires of the locals and the policy of the council. The local area is being polluted by a rubbish dump forcing the people to eventually take action against the council.

- The emotional connection comes from our desire to find out more about the main character. The author holds back information about his background which leaves questions in the reader's mind which can be explored through drama.

The session

The ideas presented are intended to be adapted and shaped by you for use in your class. They are not intended as a formula to follow or as a lesson plan. You may feel that you would like, for example, to take one idea and expand on it depending on the interests of your class or you may want to sequence a few of the ideas together. The text should help inspire teaching with a purpose which creates passion and empowers the class. This will depend, not only on the interests of your class, but also on your characteristics as a teacher. Some ideas will resonate more strongly with you than others. I hope the ideas you do use and embellish will mean that your class encounters imaginative teaching with purpose and passion for empowerment.

Connecting with the author

Gather together a range of texts by Colin Thomson. The ones which are in a similar format to *The Paperbag Prince* are *Looking For Atlantis, Ruby, How To Live Forever, The Tower to the Sun, The Paradise Garden, The Last Alchemist, Falling Angels* and *Castles*. All of these are available through Colin Thomson's website at http://colinthompson.com.

   Give the children time to look at the books, to identify the features which are similar between the texts and to talk about aspects which they like, dislike and any questions they raise. If you are able to have these texts in the school or class library over a period of time children may be able to take them home and read them for their own pleasure. By introducing the children to a range of Colin Thomson's books they will already be familiar with some of the themes and the general layout of the texts and so when you show them *The Paperbag Prince* they may be intrigued about the illustrations and will be able to find connections between this and his other texts.

Introducing the text

Put the book into a clear plastic wallet and pretend there is a padlock on the zip. Explain to the class that you are unable to access the book until a range of clues have been found. Tell them that to find the code you need to know three things from each table. Ask each table to think of something they know about the text, something they think about the text and something that they wonder about the text in the form of one question. You may need to give each table a colour photocopy of the front and back cover of the book if you don't have enough for one per table group. Once the children have had time to look at the front and back cover ask each group to report back on something they know, think and wonder about the text. If possible collect these ideas together so you can refer back to them throughout the reading of the book. Explain that they have cracked the code and the padlock can be unlocked!

Open the book to the title page and ask the children whether this helps to answer any of their questions or leads to more questions. You may want to ask where they think the man is? Why do they think he is there? What might he be thinking as he sits there? What was he doing an hour before and an hour after this point? You could use the role on the wall convention to start to build up a picture of the man in the picture. Draw an outline of the man on large paper and display it in the classroom. Explain that we are going to build up what we know, think and wonder about the man as the story progresses. Ask the class, from this picture, what kind of character they think the man has and why. Write their ideas around the outside of the outline of the man.

Reminiscing about the village

Read the first page which tells us about the beautiful green valley contrasted to the rubbish dump. Tell the children that along the green lane leading to the dump is a beautiful village which overlooks the rolling hills and outstanding scenery. Pose the question with the children wondering what the villagers would think about the dump. Ask them now to imagine that they have been a resident of the village for many years, before the dump was put there. In pairs invite the children to role play a scene from one of the kitchen tables in the village as two residents reminisce about what the village used to be like. After a few minutes stop the children and ask for any snippets of conversation which reflect the contrast between the village then and the village now. Note down some of the snippets of conversation on the flipchart. This will form a scaffold for those children who may need some support in generating ideas. Explain that as they are sat at the kitchen table they are joined by two of their neighbours and the conversation continues. Invite the children to join in groups of four and allow the role play to continue.

Next weave into your narrative some of the ideas the children have generated. Explain that the residents have got tired of the constant noise from the
lorries trundling past their houses on a daily basis. They recollect the times when
their family would come over and play in the garden breathing in the fresh air
but now when they come over they stay indoors so as not to breath in the diesel
fumes and stench coming from the dump. Set the scene with the children telling
them it is early in the morning at the weekend when they are awoken by the
sound of the lorries passing their houses. Invite the children to mime moving
over to their window, drawing back the net curtain and peering outside. Freeze
the children at this point and, as you continue the narrative, thought track some
of the thoughts of the children in role as the villagers.

Preparing the campaign

Return to the text and read up to the point where we find out that there is a
noxious pool at the rear of the dump which is oozing its destructive poison into
the surrounding area suffocating the nature. Explain that the villagers soon
found out about this and were determined to put a stop to the destruction of
their environment. Tell the children that the villagers know that the local council
meeting is taking place in the village hall and is due to end in 15 minutes. In
small groups children should work quickly in role as the villagers to produce
banners which they can use at a protest outside the village hall as the council
meeting comes to an end. Provide each group with flipchart paper and markers
for them to produce their banners. Briefly discuss how the banners might
need to be set out. Children will respond with the need for a bold statement,
maybe a visual and the use of rhyme or puns. As children get to work visit
each table prompting and supporting them in the decisions they may make.
From experience (Cremin and McDonald, 2013 p. 94) some of the statements
may be:

> We all have the hump – get rid of this dump!
> Don't be a fool – stay clear of the poison pool!
> GIVE OUR VILLAGE BACK!
> Pollution is killing us. Show us you care – clean our air!

As the 15 minutes comes to an end tell the class that the council meeting
will be over soon and we need to be ready to demonstrate outside. Organise
the children looking at the classroom door or a predetermined focal point and
encourage them to chant the statements they have on their banners. Before
the lesson ask a colleague to be prepared to come in at this point in role as the
councillor or you work as teacher in role (TiR) and to respond to the demon-
strating children by quietening them down and explaining that this is not a
suitable way to make representation to the council. Instead they can come and
see you at your surgery which takes place in the morning in the village.

'Dumpster'
Pollution Avenue
Strict Village
732 5X4

Dear Sir/Madam

I was appalled by your response to the local residents
rights and opinions, regarding the disgusting dump.
Deseases could easily be spread.
An easy touch of what kind of rubbish lay in the grotesc
dump, a child, or even an adult could be infected in an
instant.
Animals can not live in such a wasteful dump, and proberbly
wate for our actions.
Defensless in my space, I and many other villagers,
feel that you are over—rating your opinions.
Not only do we have to put up with the risk of being
infected, also, every morning the lorrys let out a
disgusting stench, wich we can not live with anymore.
I expect something to be done about this pathetic dump,
or I will go one step further.
    from

a very angry resident

Parmjot

Figure 10.1 The letter to the council from an angry resident

Meeting the councillor

Quickly organise the children into groups. You will need some children who will be in role as the councillor and others who will form groups. You may want to have family groups where children are in role as a mother, a father, an elderly grandparent and a sprightly grandchild. You may want to also have social groups. However they are organised it will be these groups who will take their representations at the surgery to the councillor. Children will need to decide which roles they will take and what their main arguments will be. Encourage them to refer back to the points made through their banners which you may want to display around the classroom as prompts.

Once the groups are decided give the groups time to decide how they want to approach the meeting. Will they be angry or diplomatic? What main point will they be making and how will they back it up? At the same time the children who are in role as the councillors will need to consider their approach. What will their stance be and what arguments will they use? After an appropriate amount of time to plan their ideas tell them that the surgery will be starting soon.

Arrange the classroom so all the meetings can take place at the same time. The children in role as the councillors should be at their desks with chairs arranged for the family groups. Each group should wait just to the side of the area while you narrate this part of the story, leading up to the point where the family group knocks on the door of the councillor's meeting room.

Watch the meetings taking place. You may want to freeze some groups at any point in order to intervene with some further ideas or to give thinking time for a response or you may wish to let the meetings run for a set amount of time before drawing them to a close. As you observe the children at work you may be able to pick out individuals who make especially convincing points or argue their case well. Once the meetings have drawn to a close gather these children together and explain that they are a new family group who are going to make their representations to the councillor at another meeting. The difference here is that the rest of the class will be an audience watching and making note of the arguments made.

Once the meetings have finished invite the children to consider which arguments were most convincing and why. In groups, or as a whole class, note down each main argument and also the supporting points relevant to each argument. Discuss which give strength and support to the arguments. Explain that as the representations to the councillors did not result in any significant changes they are going to write to their local Member of Parliament (MP). At this point model a persuasive paragraph using the main arguments and supporting points already made. Invite the children either individually or in pairs to construct their letter to their MP using the arguments from the drama.

Returning to the text explain to the children that we will find out later what the result of their campaign and letter writing has been. Read the next part of the story which tells us about the railway carriage which sits on a pile of broken bricks in the dump. On the next page we see the Paperbag Prince cycling up to the dump. We know that he makes the same journey each day but are not told much more about him at this point. Invite the children to consider what they want to know about him. The Paperbag Prince sits in his chair and animals emerge from the nooks and crannies of the dump, only the dog is shy. Return to the role on the wall which depicts the Paperbag Prince. Add any comments from the children to the role of the wall.

Exploring the character of the Paperbag Prince

Read to the point where the Paperbag Prince searches through the rubbish. Narrate this part of the story from the point of view of the Paperbag Prince noting the sorts of things he picks up and also the items he discards. Build the anticipation as you tell the children how for days, weeks, months and indeed years he has been searching for one item: one item that he lost out here all those years ago. He never really hoped that he would see it again. Then suddenly as he foraged through some old plastic bags something caught his eye. Could this be it? Narrate how he knelt down to take a closer look and reached out to touch it. Stop there and hand out a piece of plain A5 paper to each child. Invite them to draw what they think he may have found. Maybe it is the item he has been searching for or maybe it is something else. Once the children have drawn what they imagine he may have found ask them to add a caption or comment to their picture before sharing it with others in the class. The range of ideas will be interesting. Some children may think of him finding money or something he could sell whereas others may think of a more sentimental item such as a photograph or letter.

Through this activity we are finding out something about the Paperbag Prince's life which we are not told about in the text. The children will be using their imagination in order to consider the possibilities. You could take this further by exploring in more detail the item he found and building up a background story about the Paperbag Prince or you may want to continue reading the text to find out some more information.

News from the council

Read to the point where Sarah from the council comes to the rubbish dump. Her news is that the dump will be closed! Link this news back to the representations made to the council by the family groups. You may want to narrate that into this part of the story. At the end of the page Sarah says 'It's yours again . . . you can have it back'. What do the children think she means by that?

As you continue to read the text we find out a range of information to add to the role on the wall. Some of the gaps in our understanding about the Paperbag Prince are filled in but there is always a sense that we don't really get to know his inner thoughts and feelings. Read to the point where the Paperbag Prince is in bed content with life. Storytell how as he looks out of the window at his kingdom he has a feeling of accomplishment. Reaching out he takes from the shelf the item he found a few days ago in the dump, holds it close to his heart and reflects. At this point you could thought track the children to find out what his final thoughts are at this point in his life or you could invite them to note down what his reflections may be through the use of a diary which he has kept ever since his house burnt down. Children may want to write a diary entry for any point between then and now.

Make this your own

There are many opportunities to explore the power of nature and how it sometimes needs to overcome human activities. There may be environmental issues near your school which children could become involved in. Alternatively you could look at the school grounds with the children and identify areas which are in need of some attention. You could survey the school about their perceptions about the different areas and start a campaign to develop one of the areas so it is used more by the community.

*

FOOTPATH FLOWERS (2015, WALKER BOOKS) BY JON ARNO LAWSON, ILLUSTRATED BY SYDNEY SMITH

- **Possible writing opportunities**: Captions, descriptive writing, diary
- **Interactive strategies**: Freeze-frame, thought tracking, role play, improvisation
- **Age range**: 3–11

Introduction

This wordless picturebook tells the story of a girl who is walking home with her father. On the walk her father seems preoccupied with his phone call spending the majority of the walk on his mobile phone. The girl however notices the beauty of the surrounding area and is determined to spread happiness through little acts of kindness. The story reminds us to look at the world with fresh eyes, identifying the beauty in our surroundings and remembering that no act of kindness, no matter how small, is ever wasted.

Teaching objectives

- Learn to respect and, where necessary, depend upon others.
- Contribute ideas through using the imagination.
- Use questioning to seek out further information.
- Explore the variety of human emotions.
- Use a range of dramatic forms to express ideas and feelings.

Problems, emotions or challenges to be explored

- This text encourages us to consider what we value within our environment. Do we see the beauty which is in front of us or do we take it for granted?

- The difference between the outlook of the girl and her father causes us to wonder whether, as we get older, we become preoccupied with, for example, work-related issues and miss out on the simple joy we can gain from being inquisitive and noticing the people, events and nature around us.

- We are challenged to consider acts of kindness and the effect they have on people we know and equally on people we don't know. In this story no act of kindness is ever wasted. Is this true in the lives we lead?

The session

The ideas presented are intended to be adapted and shaped by you for use in your class. They are not intended as a formula to follow or as a lesson plan. You may feel that you would like, for example, to take one idea and expand on it depending on the interests of your class or you may want to sequence a few of the ideas together. The text should help inspire teaching with a purpose which creates passion and empowers the class. This will depend, not only on the interests of your class, but also on your characteristics as a teacher. Some ideas will resonate more strongly with you than others. I hope the ideas you do use and embellish will mean that your class encounters imaginative teaching with purpose and passion for empowerment.

Connecting with the theme

Talk with the children about what they consider the phrase 'acts of kindness' to mean. When have they been shown an act of kindness? What was it and how did it make them feel? Also ask when they have shown an act of kindness. What was it and how did it make them and the receiver feel? Make a list of everyday simple acts of kindness which we could all show both at home and at school. Link the acts with the feelings and emotions associated with them.

Lead the discussion on to the people who we are kind to. Are there some people it is easier to show kindness to? Children may talk about the difference between showing acts of kindness to family and friends as opposed to people who are not friends or they do not know as well. Explain that the story we are going to read is about a girl who shows acts of kindness to people as she walks home.

Introducing the text

Look at the front cover with the children. Notice the use of colour and ask why they think the girl has a red coat whereas most of the page is black and white. Discuss what they feel the intentions of the illustrator were and what effect it has on the reader?

Explain that you are going to give the children one picture from the book and they should take time to look at it, discuss what they can see and then consider what they know, what they think and also what they wonder about the story. You will need to give pictures which you think would spark possibility questioning. Maybe the start of the story, the end of the story and one act of kindness would be suitable. Children may want to note down the questions they have about the pictures. Alternatively you could give the children, in groups, a selection of the pictures from the text. You would want to give them the start and end of the story as well as one act of kindness by the girl. Hand out the sets of pictures and give the children time in groups to order the events in the story. They should then consider what they know, what they think and what they wonder about each picture. This activity will give children the chance to generate thoughts about the text and the story before you read it with them.

After giving time for children to share their ideas and talk about the possibilities within the text explain that you are going to read the story with them. Or if you have enough copies of the text let the children read the story in small groups. As this is a wordless picturebook explain that you are reading the pictures and generating ideas from them rather than being told what is happening through the text.

Reading for meaning

Read the whole book, looking carefully at each page with the children. You may want to point out certain features as you share it with the children. For example notice the importance of the birds featured in the pictures. Also talk with the children about where they think the girl was going at the end of the story. Once she has given the flowers to her mum she rushes through the garden and looks up at the birds in the sky. What is the significance of this?

Focus on the three areas of colour, story and character with the children. You could give the choice of which one each group would like to focus on or you could ask all the children to cover all three aspects.

When looking at colour, encourage the children to look at instances where colour seeps into each page. On first reading it may appear that the colour is only concentrated around the girl but as children take more notice they will see other points of colour such as the fruit and vegetable stall, the taxis and also the lady's dress at the bus stop. Ask the children to focus on what the illustrator's intentions were and also the impact of those decisions for the reader.

Retelling the story from different perspectives

The story is powerful and can be interpreted in a number of ways. Encourage children to retell the story in their own words. You could do this in a number of ways. Children could work in pairs and start to retell the story. When they need thinking time or are not sure of what to say they simply say 'change' and their partner will pick up the story. Once they want to swap they say 'change' and the story will revert to the first teller. They could repeat the process a number of times with the same or different partners. Alternatively you could set out the pictures from the first activity. Children work at retelling the story by picking a picture, retelling that part before picking the next picture in the sequence in order to retell. Eventually the whole story will have been retold.

When focusing on the characters you could ask children to retell the story from the point of view of the dad, from the point of view of the man on the bench or from the point of view of the girl. From each of these perspectives we would find something new. We can see from the illustrations that the dad is never far from the girl and, although seems preoccupied, does show an understanding of the girl's activities. From the perspective of the man on the bench it would be interesting to find out how he reacted when he woke up and whether the simple act of kindness affected him in any way. Children could possibly role play this point in the text. Lastly the children could explore what the girl is thinking at various points in the story. We can see from the outset that she is observant as she looks closely at the man's tattoo and also at the lady in the car. You could use thought bubbles throughout the story for the children to explore what the girl is thinking.

It may be tempting to ask the children to write the story which could accompany the pictures. I would be inclined to use captions instead as there is a reason why it is a wordless picturebook. You could set up an exhibition in the classroom or around the school where you frame and display each picture. Each picture could be displayed with a caption. For some pictures you may want to provide space for other children to write their own caption.

Make this your own

Use the tag line 'no act of kindness, no matter how small, is ever wasted'. Encourage the children to think about daily acts of kindness they could do. They could then promote these within the school. Make a display of an 'acts of kindness tree' which grows with the number of acts of kindness taking place. You could encourage the whole community to take part by involving parents, school governors and friends of the school.

*

LITERATURE LINKS RELATING TO THE THEME

There are many other books which explore the theme of this chapter. You may want to use them to complement the work you are doing or see how some of the drama strategies will enable you to enrich the learning experience. Suitable recommendations for use with process drama include:

The Tin Forest (2013, Templar Publishing) by Helen Ward and Wayne Anderson

Zoo (1994, Red Fox) by Anthony Browne

River Story (2015, Walker Books) by Meredith Hooper and Bee Willey

The Wump World (1999, Turtleback Books) by Bill Peet

The Curious Garden (2009, Little Brown Book Group) by Peter Brown

The Water Hole (2001, Abrams) by Graeme Base

On Meadowview Street (2007, Greenwillow Books) by Henry Cole

Just a Dream (2011, Houghton Mifflin) by Chris Van Allsburg

Owl Moon (1989, Scholastic) by J. Yolen

Farewell to Shady Glade (1981, Houghton Mifflin) by Bill Peet.

Cremin, T., & McDonald, R. (2013). Drama. In R. Jones, & D. Wyse (eds), *Creativity in the Primary Curriculum* (pp. 83–97). London: Routledge.

11 Creative ideas with texts
Overcoming fear

We are all probably afraid of something, be that being afraid of the dark, of spiders, of school or of water. Fear is an emotion which can be important for us in order to keep us safe. The fear we may feel when on a coastal walk and a strong gust of wind takes us by surprise may mean that we walk further inland ensuring we are at a safe distance from the cliffs. However other fears may hinder our lives, stopping us from being able to do things that for others would seem perfectly normal. The fear of allowing our imagination to create possibilities in our minds is a fear for some as it often results in us needing to reconsider our perceptions or the need to consider an idea or event from a new perspective. The two texts chosen here deal with different kinds of fear. The first is concerned with the fear of the unknown whereas the second deals with the fear of losing someone close to us.

THE KRAKEN (2001, LOTHIAN CHILDREN'S BOOKS) BY GARY CREW AND MARC MCBRIDE

- **Possible writing opportunities**: Poetry
- **Interactive strategies**: Improvisation, freeze-frame, thought tracking
- **Age range**: 9–11

Introduction

The Kraken is a legend which tells of a giant sea monster which inhabits the seas around Norway and Greenland. It has featured in a range of texts but is brought to life vividly by Gary Crew who tells the tale of two children who sit together at the end of the jetty. Christopher is blind although there is no physiological reason for this and it could be said that Antonia is blind to Christopher's imagination. This is a story about the importance of using our imagination, of looking with fresh eyes at the world around us and not taking things for granted.

Teaching objectives

- Develop willingness to accept and respect the ideas of others and to build on them.
- Identify with characters and actions through role playing.
- Contribute ideas through using the imagination.

- Learn how to work together to solve human and practical problems.
- Use a range of dramatic forms to express ideas and feelings.
- Realise that the views of individuals do not always coincide.

Problems, emotions or challenges to be explored

- The mystery surrounding the existence of the Kraken will pose a challenge for the children and will create intrigue. Links to other legends can be made and work could be undertaken to look for facts and opinions about each legionary creature.
- The emotional connection will be made with Christopher. Christopher uses his imagination to see the world around him whereas Antonia seems averse to looking at the world from his perspective.
- The challenge for the reader is to consider which parts of the story are taking place in the imagination and which are actual events happening to the characters in the story.

The session

The ideas presented are intended to be adapted and shaped by you for use in your class. They are not intended as a formula to follow or as a lesson plan. You may feel that you would like, for example, to take one idea and expand on it depending on the interests of your class or you may want to sequence a few of the ideas together. The text should help inspire teaching with a purpose which creates passion and empowers the class. This will depend, not only on the interests of your class, but also on your characteristics as a teacher. Some ideas will resonate more strongly with you than others. I hope the ideas you do use and embellish will mean that your class encounters imaginative teaching with purpose and passion for empowerment.

Connecting with the text

Spend time before introducing the book to the children exploring various legends from the sea. The mysterious nature of some of the legends and myths creates curiosity and raises questions which children will be keen to explore. You could investigate mermaids, the Bermuda Triangle, the Loch Ness Monster, the Mary Celeste and finally the Kraken.

The Kraken is a fascinating legend which features in different folklore and has also starred in the film *Pirates of the Caribbean*. It has been described as being like a giant squid or like an octopus although older descriptions point to the Kraken being more like a crab. The many armed creature would be feared by sailors as it was believed that it could reach up out of the sea and engulf any ship which passed through its waters. Show a range of pictures to the class of depictions of the Kraken giving time for them to look carefully at its features. In groups ask children to describe the Kraken. You could encourage the use of similes which could then be put together to form a class poem.

Introducing the text

Explain that the book you are going to share with the class is called *The Kraken* and is by Gary Crew and Marc McBride. Tell them that there are two children in the story who enjoy spending the summer going down and sitting on the jetty. Without showing the front cover ask children to draw what illustration they would expect to see on the front cover. Make sure they have all the features expected such as the authors, title and publisher. Through the drawing of the front cover children will be making predictions about the possible events which may take place in the text. Share some of the front covers in order to talk about the predictions before showing the actual front cover. What surprises the children? Does it meet with their expectations?

Read the first page while displaying the illustration and contrast the imagination of Christopher to the reality of Antonia. What does this tell us about the characters? Are we surprised that Antonia tells Christopher the reality of the jetty being a row of rotting pylons and splintery planks?

Seeing but not seeing

Read the start of the next page where Antonia explains that for people who can see, although the world is beautiful 'sometimes we stop seeing it'. Discuss with the class what they think this means. What, in their immediate environment, do the children think they may have 'stopped seeing'? If possible take the class on a 'look afresh' walk around the school and the school grounds. Stop at certain predetermined points to look again at the surroundings and note aspects which may, until now, have gone unnoticed. Children could produce 'have you noticed?' or 'look again' notices to encourage other people to look at the environment with a fresh outlook.

At the end of the page Antonia tells Christopher that she thinks that he is the lucky one as he can make the world as fresh and beautiful as he wants it to be. This is an interesting perspective but shows how we can look at the positives in a range of situations. Continue reading to the point where Antonia discusses imagination. Ask the class what they perceive imagination to be. Work towards the definition of imagination being able to see the possible rather than the actual. Play some games with the children seeing if they can create possibilities for a range of objects. For example you may ask them to think of ten uses for a brick, or ten uses for a piece of paper. Develop this by moving away from objects to using pictures and asking children to discuss the possibilities associated with the picture.

Questioning in role

At the end of the page it is clear that Christopher wants to ask Antonia something which is on his mind. Consider with the children the questions which Christopher may want to ask.

Read on to the point where Antonia asks Christopher to describe the jetty to her from his imagination. Pre-prepare a range of objects which you have at the front of the class in bags or shoe boxes. Tell the children that you would like a volunteer to come and choose a box or bag. They will need to put their hand in, feel what is there and describe it to the rest of the class. While the description is given the rest of the children need to draw what they imagine the object could be. Once this has been demonstrated with the whole class you may want to give the opportunity for the same activity to be undertaken in groups.

Read on to the point where Christopher asks Antonia to join him in the pearl boat. Invite the children to form pairs taking the role of the two children. The child taking Christopher's role will convince Antonia to trust him and set foot in the boat. The child taking Antonia's role will need to question and test Christopher in order to be convinced to step into the boat. While the role play is taking place note down, either on card or on the flipchart, some of the doubts voiced by Antonia. Also ask the children to note down the doubts heard on sticky notes.

Generating poetry

Read the next page which describes the Kraken lurking under the jetty feeding on any doubts. The children will have voiced some of the doubts in the role play. Explain that you are going to build a class poem about the doubts which are feeding the Kraken. Explain that you have adapted a couple of lines from the text which will form the chorus of the poem:

> The Kraken that feeds on doubt,
> The Kraken that thrives on fear.

Now use some of the ideas noted down from the role play documenting Antonia's doubt. Explain that you will read them out, and in-between each doubt the class should chorus:

> The Kraken that feeds on doubt,
> The Kraken that thrives on fear.

Then experiment with reordering the doubts with the class. Will the poem sound better if the doubts are read in a different order? It could be that the doubts could be reordered to start small and build into bigger doubts. At the same time the chorus could get louder representing the Kraken getting stronger and rising from the depths of the sea.

Once this has been modelled to the class allow children time to work on their own poem using their doubts from the role play. If they have written the doubts on the sticky notes they will be able to reorder them and experiment with the sound of the poem. They may want to create their own chorus. Choose some children who would like to perform the poem. Display the chorus to the whole class and ask how they would like this read. For example would they like it read quietly at first, building the volume or would they like it read slowly at first then quickening the pace?

Exploring the intentions of the Kraken

Read on to where we are told that the children's mother was preparing the evening meal. Focus on the part which describes the doubts she felt about Christopher's recovery. The dramatic illustrations by Marc McBride will stimulate a range of discussion by the children about the perceived intentions for the Kraken. We are told how the Kraken, taking human form, interacts with first the children's mother and then their father. There are various comments he makes to the parents which would indicate a degree of menace and make us fearful of the children's fate. Read to the point where the Kraken says: "Gone," she answered with a croak. "Both gone. Like yours."

Ask the children to consider the point the Kraken is talking about. Where might they have gone? Is he speaking literally or metaphorically? Invite the children, in groups, to form a freeze-frame of the moment when the children had 'both gone'. Through the freeze-frame they will be exploring their ideas for the possibilities surrounding the clues given by the Kraken. After giving the opportunity for the children to discuss their opinions ask the groups to create their freeze-frame. If the children are used to this convention ask one child to lead the rest of the class around the freeze-frame. The child should explain what the idea is and how the text has led them to this freeze-frame. It would be great if the child could also thought track some of the thoughts of the characters in the freeze-frame.

The parents' panic

Read on to the point where both parents are running towards the sea looking for their children. Gary Crew helps us visualise this scene and creates a sense of urgency and uncertainty. Use a chair to represent the parents' thoughts and invite the class to form a circle around the chair. Storytell the point in the text where the parents run from their different directions and catch each other's eye. They call to each other raising their concerns although at first their words are lost in the wind. Explain that we want to capture some of the thoughts and comments at this point. Model stepping out of the circle, touching the chair and speaking one of the thoughts or comments from either the mother or the father. Give time for the children to also speak the thoughts of the parents before continuing with the story.

At the end we find that the children are safe and the Kraken sinks back into the murky depths of the sea.

Make this your own

I wonder where the Kraken goes next! As it sinks into the murky depths and listens out for the doubts of the world where will it surface? Maybe it can hear the conversations taking place on a nearby ship or maybe it makes its way to one of the piers around the coastline listening and waiting until it can make its move. You could explore the possibilities with children as they develop their own stories about the next encounter with the Kraken.

*

DEATH IN A NUT (2005, FRANCES LINCOLN CHILDREN'S BOOKS) BY ERIC MADDERN, ILLUSTRATED BY PAUL HESS

- **Possible writing opportunities**: Story generated from an oral retelling
- **Interactive strategies**: Drawing, decision alley, hot seating, role play
- **Age range**: 7–11

Introduction

Originating from the great Scottish storyteller Duncan Williamson, *Death in a Nut* is a visual retelling of the traditional story. The structural markers throughout lead the reader to associate the story with the folklore, fairytale and oral tradition genres with the opening line of 'Once upon a time there was a lad called Jack who lived with his mother in a cottage by the sea' linking to other similar story starts in the reader's mind.

The story begins by introducing Jack and his mother who live in a cottage by the sea. One day Jack's mother becomes ill and tells Jack that she may die. Distraught by the news, a tear-filled Jack walks his familiar route along the coastal path until he sees a figure walking towards him. We are told that the figure is death himself on his way to visit Jack's mother. This leads Jack to take action against death in order to save his mother. As the story unfolds we see the repercussions of Jack's actions and how he is tested until finally he returns to the spot by the sea near the cottage where the story began to make amends for what he has done.

Jack's enlightening journey highlights the realisation that without death there can be no life.

Teaching objectives

- Use questioning to seek out further information.
- Contribute ideas through using the imagination.
- Learn to respect and, where necessary, depend upon others.
- Explore the variety of human emotions.
- Identify with characters and actions through role playing.
- Have the confidence and ability to put across a particular point of view.

Problems, emotions or challenges to be explored

- The emotional connection within this story relates to our perceptions of death. This can be a difficult topic and may challenge us as teachers but choosing texts which deal with the issue sensitively can help us discuss it with openness, supportiveness and understanding.

The session

The ideas presented are intended to be adapted and shaped by you for use in your class. They are not intended as a formula to follow or as a lesson plan.

You may feel that you would like, for example, to take one idea and expand on it depending on the interests of your class or you may want to sequence a few of the ideas together. The text should help inspire teaching with a purpose which creates passion and empowers the class. This will depend, not only on the interests of your class, but also on your characteristics as a teacher. Some ideas will resonate more strongly with you than others. I hope the ideas you do use and embellish will mean that your class encounters imaginative teaching with purpose and passion for empowerment.

Connecting with the theme

This was originally an oral story so this session will work towards children being able to retell the story.

This text is a brilliant source of understanding and logical reasoning surrounding the concept of death. Dealing with an issue which we, as humans, often find difficult will need careful planning and consideration from the teacher. This text will lead to some thought-provoking questions and so could suit inclusion within an RE or PSHE lesson. Alternatively you may wish to include this text alongside other texts dealing with the same issue (some of which are included in the literature links section).

Children may have some preconceived ideas about a book which has the subject of death as its theme. You could talk to the children (before showing them the book) about what we would expect from a picturebook about death. It may be suitable for children to think or draw what they imagine might be on the front cover. These perceptions of death can then be explored.

Before reading the story explore the issue of death with the children. This could be done by looking at the front cover of the book and talking about the title. Through the picture on the front cover children may assume that the book is about an animal dying. They may also think that it has a degree of comedy through the way the hen is moving away from the title. Compare the front cover with their own drawings or thoughts about what they expected from the front cover.

Introducing the text

Show the children the double-page spread before the title page which shows a vast expanse of beach leading into the sea. In the distance beneath the hills we see a lone figure. In the foreground of the right-hand page is a solitary crab. Discuss with the children their interpretations of the significance of the space between the two figures.

Explain that the figure in the distance is a character called Jack who lives near the sea with his mother. Tell the class that Jack often walks along the beach and enjoys finding things which have been washed up. Give a couple of suggestions and then ask the children to think of what sort of items he could find. Make a list of the items and ask the children what Jack might do with them? What could he make?

Jack's first encounter with death

Read the first two pages with the children and compare the list of items Jack found on the beach to the list the children have thought of. What do they think Jack would make with the items he found? From the first two pages ask the children what sort of character they think Jack has and what their reasons are for thinking this. What events in his life might have moulded his character?

Read to the point where Jack meets death. Ask children to listen to the description and to imagine what they think the picture might look like. Show them the picture and ask whether it is similar or different from what they imagined. Why do they think the illustrator has drawn death like this?

Read to the point when Jack has smashed the scythe and death says 'Young man, you've done it now'. What do we expect will happen? Children may think that death will bring some devastating course of events to Jack but instead death gets smaller and smaller as Jack hits death again and again until 'at last Jack had him in the palm of his hand'. Ask the children what they would do if they had death in the palm of their hand?

Continue reading the story stopping to ask questions and identify significant points within the story such as the point where Jack realised that the events taking place were a result of what he had done. Jack needs to release death from the nut as his mother has instructed him. At this point it may be pertinent to explore Jack's conflicting thoughts through a decision alley.

The end of death?

Discuss with the children the decision Jack needs to make. What would be the advantages and disadvantages of letting death out? Invite the children to come and form two lines in the classroom facing each other. Decide who would like to be in role as Jack and then as he makes his way through the 'alley' or 'corridor' he will hear his thoughts voiced by the other children. Once he has walked through and heard the various thoughts and advice ask the other children to sit down so Jack can then share what decision he would make based on what he has heard.

Retelling the story

Read to the end of the story. Explain that we are going to work on retelling the story so give the children some time to reflect on the main events they can remember. Ask the children to get into pairs. Explain that this retelling will be based on what they can initially remember. The children decide who will go first. The first child starts to retell the story. At any point they can say 'change' and their partner takes over the retelling until they say 'change'. After a short period of time they will have retold their initial memories of the story.

After the initial retelling ask the children, in small groups, to think of five main events in the story. They may want to record these at this stage. This could be through a story map or possibly a story hand, whichever they prefer.

The children can then use the story map or story hand to retell the story again with their partner. Afterwards talk with the children about whether the pictorial representation helped or hindered them? Did they rely on it too much or were they able to use it as a prompt.

Model the retelling of the whole story to the rest of the class yourself by using a story map or story hand which you have made. Ask the children which part of the story they could visualise most vividly. What was it about the story-telling which allowed for this? It could be a connection to their own experiences or it may relate to their own favourite part of the story from their retelling. In what ways could other parts of the retelling be improved? Allowing the children to comment on your own retelling and the way you model the constructive nature of the conversation will allow children to repeat this in another retelling of their own to a different member of the class.

Children need as many opportunities as possible to retell the story and to develop their story map or story hand. They will be able to use the skills they have learnt and adapt them to other storytelling.

*

LITERATURE LINKS RELATING TO THE THEME

There are many other books which explore the theme of this chapter. You may want to use them to complement the work you are doing or see how some of the drama strategies will enable you to enrich the learning experience. Suitable recommendations for use with process drama include:

Grandpa (2003, Red Fox) by John Burningham

What If (2014, Picture Corgi) by Anthony Browne

The Rumor (2011, Creative Editions) by Monique Felix

Duck, Death and the Tulip (2008, Gecko Press) by Wolf Erlbruch

The Red Tree (2010, Hodder Children's Books) by Shan Tan

Darkness Slipped In (2014, Macmillan Children's Books) by Ella Burfoot

The Huge Bag of Worries (2011, Hodder Children's Books) by Virginia Ironside and Frank Rodgers

Daredevil Duck (2015, Running Press Kids) by Charlie Alder

Brave Irene (2011, Particular Books) by William Steig

The Dark (2014, Orchard Books) by Lemony Snicket

Courage (2002, Walter Lorraine Books) by Bernard Waber

Max the Brave (2015, Puffin) by Ed Vere

Old Pig (2009, Allen and Unwin) by Margaret Wild and Ron Brooks.

12 Creative ideas with texts
Possessions and obsessions

Do you know people who you might term as 'materialistic'? I expect that by that term we mean people who put material needs in life ahead of emotional needs. It is, of course, difficult as it could be argued that material objects are a necessity in life and part of our joy comes from interaction with them. I suppose it is at the point when the object becomes a possession which causes an obsession that we could say that a shift in focus is needed. The two texts chosen here deal with this issue in very different ways. The first focuses on the difficulties which arise when people become obsessed with something which stops them from doing all the activities which up until now they enjoyed. The second text shows that through conformity we might expect people to want to have a range of possessions because it is 'normal' but in this story the girl wants nothing more than to be free in the wild.

THE WRETCHED STONE (1991, HOUGHTON MIFFLIN) WRITTEN AND ILLUSTRATED BY CHRIS VAN ALLSBURG

- **Possible writing opportunities**: Persuasive writing, diary entry, newspaper account, descriptive writing

- **Interactive strategies**: Storytelling, freeze-frame, drawing, role play, improvisation, thought tracking

- **Age range**: 7–11

Introduction

The Wretched Stone is a story told in the form of a captain's log charting the voyage of the *Rita Anne* as it sailed the seas. Written by Chris Van Allsburg we join the crew on an adventure into uncharted waters. The crew, who have been assembled for the latest voyage of the *Rita Anne*, are accomplished storytellers, dancers and musicians but all that changes when they bring on board something they discovered on an uncharted island. Chris Van Allsburg captures the tense nature of the dilemma the captain finds himself in as he grapples with the crew who are transfixed by the object and useless to him. Suspense builds as the *Rita Anne* turns into choppy waters and the captain has a decision to make in order to save himself and the crew.

Teaching objectives

- Contribute ideas through using the imagination.
- Learn to respect and, where necessary, depend upon others.
- Explore the differences between right and wrong in simple moral dilemmas posed through drama.
- Use questioning to seek out further information.
- Explore the variety of human emotions.
- Create and take part in improvised scenes in order to explore particular issues which could, for instance, have a practical, social or moral dimension.
- Gain confidence in their own abilities, particularly to communicate verbally and non-verbally.

Problems, emotions or challenges to be explored

- The first problem is the fact that the island which can be seen from the ship is not marked on any map. This causes curiosity and raises a number of questions which need answering.
- The second issue is the object that the sailors have brought on board. What is the power it has over the men? Why are they so entranced by it?
- The challenge is to do with needing to save the ship from near certain destruction as the captain tries to sail it alone through the storm. Something needs to change in order for all the men to survive.

The session

The ideas presented are intended to be adapted and shaped by you for use in your class. They are not intended as a formula to follow or as a lesson plan. You may feel that you would like, for example, to take one idea and expand on it depending on the interests of your class or you may want to sequence a few of the ideas together. The text should help inspire teaching with a purpose which creates passion and empowers the class. This will depend, not only on the interests of your class, but also on your characteristics as a teacher. Some ideas will resonate more strongly with you than others. I hope the ideas you do use and embellish will mean that your class encounters imaginative teaching with purpose and passion for empowerment.

Making connections with the text

Make sure you have covered over the title of the book so children cannot see the words 'Wretched Stone'. You may want to show some pictures of various water vessels and ask children to comment on similarities and differences. What are their purposes and who would travel on them? Ask the children what other vessels could be added to the collection. If you have shown a canoe, a battleship, a raft and a dinghy the children may suggest adding a sailing ship and a cruise liner for example. Collect together children's experience of any of these types of vessels. Some children may, for example have been to visit HMS Victory or had the opportunity to go sailing. Encourage the children to first think from their own perspective and then from the perspective of someone else on one of the vessels. You could put one of the pictures into context at this point and give it a time in history for the children to consider.

Introducing the text

Show the title page which says 'Excerpts from the log of the *Rita Anne*. Randall Ethan Hope, Captain'. Explain that sometimes the captain of a ship would record the voyage by noting the events in a log. You could talk to the children about the similarities and differences between a log and a diary. Give the children time to look at this page. You may want to discuss what the word 'excerpts' means and why they think only excerpts have been included.

Sailors' stories

Read up to and including the entry for May 17th where we are told that the sailors often relieve the boredom by telling tales of past adventures. At this point tell the children your own tale, in role as one of the sailors, about a past adventure. While telling your story ask questions and give prompts to the children such as 'Maybe this happened to you', 'Did any other sailors also see the . . .?' At a pertinent point in your story stop and invite the children to start to think about their tale of past adventure before you draw them back together and conclude your story. Use the space in the classroom to depict the deck of the ship. Children will be in role as the crew maybe relaxing in the calm weather. Encourage children to walk around the deck until you clap your hands. On that signal they should go to the closest person and tell them their story of past adventure. You could possibly repeat the process about three times.

The mysterious land

Continue to read the June 5th extract. Discuss the fact that the land has not been charted on any map. What do the children think the reason may be for this? Invite children to offer a range of possibilities. Explain that the crew were disconcerted by this discovery and the mood changed on the ship from one of stories of past adventure to one of stories of imminent danger. Tell the children that the captain decided to anchor the ship just off the south coast of the island. The crew could easily see the island in the distance. Explain that as the sailors went to bed that night they started to dream about what may confront them on the island the next morning. Invite the children, in groups, to think about one event from their dream to depict as a freeze-frame. It could be the point where the crew find something, see something or hear something intriguing on the island. After a short discussion time invite the children to decide on a caption for their freeze-frame. Count down from five to zero when the groups should freeze. Storytell the events of that night as the crew went to bed anticipating the day ahead. Tell how as they drifted off to sleep their dreams turned to the

an animal
we think a
cross between a
baby and an
octopus – it seems
friendly, curious,
but may be a
bad omen.

Figure 12.1 Imagining what might have been found

Green
Stones

A big brown box with a leaf
shaped hole on it and one
one leaf from that island
opens the box.

Figure 12.2 Imagining what might have been found

events to come. Then go round the freeze-frames in turn asking groups to insert the caption of the freeze-frame into your narrative. For example you may say 'the first event was a premonition of . . . followed by the anticipation of . . .' The aim is to build the freeze-frames into the narrative of the tale being told.

Continue reading the excerpt from June 6th to the point where it says 'we also discovered something quite extraordinary, which I have brought aboard'. At this point children should use A5 paper already on their desks to draw what they think could be the extraordinary item. You may want to pose some possibilities to support the children or see what they imagine themselves. It would be beneficial for you to also draw what you imagine might be discovered. After a short period of time display your example on a visualiser if possible and say that you want to write a phrase to create intrigue about your drawing. Invite the children to do the same with their drawing before giving the opportunity for some children to share their possibilities.

Bringing the rock aboard

Read the next part of the June 6th entry which tells us that, at the captain's discretion, the rock was brought aboard the ship. The entry tells us that six strong men were required to lift the stone. Choose six children (they do not need to be either male or strong!) to recreate this scene. You may want to be one of the crew yourself to direct the scene as teacher in role. Gather the crew together and tell them that the captain wants you to bring the rock aboard. Start to ask the other crew what they think about that decision. Make sure they talk quietly so the captain does not hear. Your aim is to put doubt in the crew's mind about why the rock is being brought aboard. Together, with the participants, role play picking the rock up. After a few steps freeze the scene and explain that you are going to tap some crew on the shoulder and they should speak what they think about the decision to bring the rock aboard the ship.

The power of the rock

Continue to read the excerpts from June 10th and June 13th to the point where it says 'I told Mr Howard that tomorrow I will have the thing thrown over-board'. Extend this scene by inviting the children to form pairs, with one taking the role of Mr Howard and the other taking the role of the captain. Ensure the children understand the reasons and motives of each for wanting to keep the rock or throw it overboard before entering into a quick role play. Explain that the captain had met Mr Howard on the deck of the ship where he confronted him about the rock. Count down from five to one. When you get to one, all the children taking the role of the captain should tell their partner (Mr Howard) what their concerns are before Mr Howard responds. Allow the role play to run for a couple of minutes before stopping. Ask the children who were in role as Mr Howard whether they heard any good arguments from the captain? You could note these on a flipchart to form a scaffold for the children. Then ask the children in role as the captain if they heard any convincing arguments from Mr Howard. Again note these on the flipchart. Once you have gathered a range of responses, together with the children, look at the ideas noted on the flipchart and see if you could adapt and change the language to make it more convincing or persuasive.

Repeat the role play but this time in groups of four where two children will be the captain and two children will be Mr Howard. Children could refer to the ideas on the flipchart to support their thinking if they would like to or may use it as a starting point to embellish further. After a short period of time stop the children and again ask for any examples of convincing and persuasive arguments from the groups. Draw the conversation together by saying that the meeting did not go well as Mr Howard went back to the crew to tell them of the captain's plan!

The captain's dilemma

Read the excerpt from June 14th and the first part of June 15th which tells us of the storm which the *Rita Anne* has sailed into. The captain is struggling on deck by himself. Create the scene in the classroom. You may want to use some soundscape clips to create the stormy atmosphere. Tell the children that the storm is getting worse with every minute. Invite the children to take the role of the captain and find some space in the classroom. The idea will be to create the frantic nature of the scene on the ship as the winds pick up and the captain becomes even more desperate. In a similar way to the game 'Simon Says' call out a range of actions for the children to act out such as 'pulling in the canvas', 'steading the steering', 'holding on to the deck', 'bailing out the water' and 'taking cover'. You could start slowly and then build the pace of change until you suddenly freeze the scene. It works well if at the same moment you freeze the scene the music abruptly stops as well. This creates a quiet space, frozen in time, where we can explore the captain's thoughts.

There are a number of ways to explore what the captain is thinking. You could hear the thoughts from the captain by indicting to the children that they should speak his thoughts at this time. Alternatively you could have an object symbolising the *Rita Anne* and asking the children to form a circle around it. The object could be as simple as a chair. Once the circle is formed you should storytell the events of the night stating how the captain felt for sure that this would be his, and the crew's, last night aboard the ship before it is battered by the force of the storm, broken and sinks to the depths of the sea. In this frozen moment his thoughts turn to his hopes, wishes and aspirations. Invite the children, in turn, to step forward and touch the chair. As they touch it they should speak out the captain's thoughts at this time.

Once the children have shared their thoughts explain that the captain was desperate and knew that he needed the support of the crew. Return to the text (without showing the picture) and read the part which says: 'This is, I am sure, my last entry. What I have seen is so horrifying I barely have the strength to write it down. After I pounded at the door to the forward hold, it finally swung open.' Question the children about what could be so horrifying before giving them time to complete this diary entry.

Excerpt from the log of the Rita Anne

RANDALL ETHAN HOPE

CAPTAIN

June 15th

This is, I am sure, my last entry. What I have just seen is so horrifying I barely have the strength to write it down. After I pounded at the door to the forward hatch, it finally swung open.

I couldn't believe my eyes. The rock had grown bigger and all the crew around it was laying on the floor. I wasn't sure if they were dead or just knocked out lying on the floor. But I knew whatever had happened to the crew was soon surely going to happen to me. I was scared. I didn't know what was going to happen to me. Maybe the crews souls had been sucked out and turned into ghosts and them ghosts will probably try to do something to me. They are probably taking all the stregnth strenth out of me so I wasn't able to escape or try to find help. Whatever was going to happen to me I knew it was going to be bad.

Figure 12.3 Possibly the captain's last entry

The last hope

After reading and sharing some of the children's ideas show them the picture of the crew transformed into apes and read the rest of the excerpt from June 15th. Ask the children why they think the crew have turned into apes. What do they think the apes may symbolise?

Read to the end of the book which tells us that the crew have landed in the harbour town of Santa Pango. Draw the links with the children between the rock and the effect it had on the crew, taking away their human characteristics and regressing them to apes, and the symbolism it may evoke. Discuss what, in our modern time, may take the place of the rock. This could lead on to a range of work based around personal social and health education exploring a range of addictions and their effects.

Make this your own

You could extend the drama further by setting up the scenario that the captain's actions to scuttle the *Rita Anne* were not met with pleasure from his superiors when the crew returned back to land. In fact they decided to hold an internal disciplinary in order to demote the captain for his actions. You could recreate the court scene with the children with the 'prosecution' and 'defence'. The dilemma is that the crew have vowed never to speak of the events aboard the *Rita Anne* and so the children will need to decide how the crew will support the captain without breaking their word.

*

WILD (2015, FLYING EYE BOOKS) BY EMILY HUGHES

- **Possible writing opportunities**: Instructions
- **Interactive strategies**: Sense splat, role play, thought tracking, emotion graph, forum theatre, decision alley
- **Age range**: 5–9

Introduction

This story is about a child who does not want to conform to the expectations of what may be deemed 'normal' life, instead she enjoys being free in the wild exploring and interacting with nature. The bird, bear and fox taught her what she needed to know in order to survive until one night when there were some new animals in the forest, some humans, who took her away and gave her to a couple who thought they knew how to look after her. In time it is clear that the girl is not happy and could not conform to this new way of life. She needed to be free and in the end everyone knew it was right for her to be free.

Teaching objectives

- Contribute ideas through using the imagination.
- Use questioning to seek out further information.
- Identify with characters and actions through role playing.
- Explore the differences between right and wrong in simple moral dilemmas posed through drama.
- Have the confidence and ability to put across a particular point of view.
- Realise that the views of individuals do not always coincide.

Problems, emotions or challenges to be explored

- The main issue in this text concerns the need for conformity in society. Children will know that for an institution, such as school, to function there needs to be agreement from the members of the institution regarding conformity. However this text will challenge that notion and look at the needs and desires of an individual who is forced to conform by people who are supposedly experts in the field.

The session

The ideas presented are intended to be adapted and shaped by you for use in your class. They are not intended as a formula to follow or as a lesson plan. You may feel that you would like, for example, to take one idea and expand on it depending on the interests of your class or you may want to sequence a few of the ideas together. The text should help inspire teaching with a purpose which creates passion and empowers the class. This will depend, not only on the interests of your class, but also on your characteristics as a teacher. Some ideas will resonate more strongly with you than others. I hope the ideas you do use and embellish will mean that your class encounters imaginative teaching with purpose and passion for empowerment.

Connecting with the theme

Discuss with the class the different rules you have in the class and in the school. Talk about the reasons for these and the idea of conformity. Talk with the children about the advantages and disadvantages of having to conform. Ask if any children find it difficult and to explain which aspects are hard for them. What would happen if no one needed to conform?

Introducing the text

Introduce the text by showing the front cover. Give children time to talk about what they notice. Ask them to think of one phrase which might summarise the character of the girl. Then show the class the image on the title page which shows a contrasting expression. Ask the class to think of words or a phrase to describe the girl. What could have happened in order for the difference in expression to occur?

Read up to the point where the text says 'And she understood, and was happy'. Look at what evidence we have for her being happy. Children should use the pictures to justify their opinions. Ask the children if they think that they would be happy in a similar environment. How long do they think they would enjoy being in a similar environment? Compare the environment in the text to their own environment at home. This could be done through the use of a giant class Venn diagram.

At home in your surroundings

Look at the illustration where the girl is contentedly sat at the base of the tree surrounded by animals. Give each group a copy of the illustration and encourage them to consider what it is like through the exploration of her senses. You may want to use different colour sticky notes to denote the senses and ask children to write down what they think the girl would see, hear, smell, taste, touch and also to note down what her feelings would be at this point. This can then be compared with a similar activity later in the text where she is in different surroundings. Collect the ideas together and together write a shared piece showing the peaceful and contented nature of this illustration.

When others think they know best

Show the next illustration and read the accompanying text 'One day she met some new animals in the forest . . .' Explore the illustration with the class. They will note that the girl has been trapped. They will also recognise that her expression is more one of sadness and anger than fear. In addition the humans look upset and, in a way, sorrowful for the girl as if they know that she will not like what they are going to do. At this point use the forum theatre convention to create this scene in the class. Invite a child to take the role of the girl and invite two other children to take the role of the captors. You may want other children to be outside the scene to voice the thoughts of the animals (who do not appear in the illustration). Ask the children to take their positions at the front of the class and ask the rest of the children to offer suggestions for how they should appear. Encourage them to be specific with their language so instead of saying 'the girl will look angry' ask them to describe the action and facial features which would show the observer that she was angry. Create the scene and then freeze it in order to thought track the characters. It could be interesting to find out first of all what the characters might say and then what they might be thinking.

Read the next page and show the double-page spread of the girl being taken away in the car. Again look at the expression and discuss why the dog may be sitting at the rear of the truck. Explain that as the truck drove away the other animals emerged from their place of hiding. Explore what the children think the other animals may be thinking.

Exploring emotions

Explore the next double page. Notice how the people who came to get the girl are not the same people looking after her. Discuss with the children what this could symbolise. The couple now looking after the girl are perceived as 'experts' and there are many clues which allude to this in the room. The note on the table possibly refers to the girl as a specimen. At this point ask the children to predict what the outcome might be. Why do they think this and what elements would need to be present for an alternative outcome?

Read on to where we are told 'And she did not understand, and she was not happy'. Notice how the illustrations have a border now giving the impression of entrapment whereas previously, in the forest, there was a sense of freedom. Look at the illustration of the girl sat on the floor and consider how her feelings have changed over time. Use an emotion graph to show how the girl's feelings have changed. Draw two axes, using the horizontal axis to mark significant points in the story and the vertical axis for emotion. Then go through the story and plot the emotions of the girl at each point. This could be developed by adding annotations to describe the reasons for the emotions. Once a class or group emotion graph has been completed invite the children to use it to retell the story from the point of view of the girl.

Once the emotions have been explored and the story retold a few times from the girl's perspective, consider with the class the choices the girl has at this point. She could stay and work to conform or possibly escape and return to where she felt happiest. Consider the advantages and disadvantages of both outcomes. Use the drama convention of 'decision alley' which is also sometimes known as the 'thought tunnel' or 'conscience corridor' to give children the opportunity to voice the girl's thoughts. Invite children to form two lines facing each other in the classroom. Choose one child to take on the role of the girl. She will slowly walk down the corridor listening to the conflict in her own mind voiced by the children forming the lines. Once she has walked the corridor give her time to consider what she has heard and then decide on her course of action.

Concluding the drama

Read on to where we see the girl leaving the house riding on the back of the dog. Notice how the dog now looks happy and relieved as if he understood the entrapment the girl was feeling. The illustration contrasts the greyness and unhappiness of the buildings with the colour and happiness of the forest. Read the final page and discuss with the children the meaning of the last line. Also talk about the reasons why they feel the story ends with an ellipsis.

Make this your own

Develop the theme by identifying rules which must be kept and rules which can be broken. This will lead to an interesting philosophical discussion about who sets the rules and what gives that person/those people the right to set the rules. You could look at examples where the rules need to be broken in order to develop. With older children you could also introduce the concept of colonialism and make links between colonial actions and the text.

*

LITERATURE LINKS RELATING TO THE THEME

There are many other books which explore the theme of this chapter. You may want to use them to complement the work you are doing or see how some of the drama strategies will enable you to enrich the learning experience. Suitable recommendations for use with process drama include:

The Stranger (1986, Houghton Mifflin) by Chris Van Allsburg

The Arrival (2014, Hodder Children's books) by Shaun Tan

The Rabbits (2010, Hodder Children's books) by Shaun Tan

The Little Gardener (2015, Flying Eye Books) by Emily Hughes

Imelda and the Goblin King (2015, Flying Eye Books) by Briony May Smith

Louis I, King of the Sheep (2015, Enchanted Lion Books) by Olivier Tallec

Enormous Smallness (2015, Enchanted Lion Books) by Di Giacomo and Matthew Burgess

On a Beam of Light (2013, Chronicle) by Jennifer Berne.

13 Creative ideas with texts
Dreams

Can you remember the last dream you had? We are told that we all dream whether we remember them or not. Our mind conjures up images which together with our senses can take us on tremendous journeys or sometimes to places we would not usually be brave enough to enter. I wonder whether we use the notion of dreams within the classroom and explore the stories which are formed each night. There is certainly potential to step into the imaginative experiences and identify the images which are made by our minds. A starting point could be the two texts chosen in this section. The first is about a boy who, for the first time, experiences a bad dream and needs to forge his own courage to overcome the dark things of the night. The second text focuses on the point before we wake up, that moment when we are comfortable in bed and wish that the night would go on for ever!

THE BOY AND THE CLOTH OF DREAMS (1994, WALKER BOOKS) BY JENNY KORALEK, ILLUSTRATED BY JAMES MAYHEW

- **Possible writing opportunities**: Poetry, descriptive writing
- **Interactive strategies**: storytelling, freeze-frame, hot seating, decision alley
- **Age range**: 5–9

Introduction

In the style of a contemporary fairytale this is a story about a boy coming of age and facing his fear of the dark. The only item that until now had kept the dark night things away was his precious blanket which he kept with him each night. Unfortunately the boy trips on his cloth which causes it to rip, no longer protecting him from the night. When he arrives at his grandmother's house she sees the tear and knows that this is the night when her grandson will need to face his darkest fears and, with her encouragement, overcome them.

Teaching objectives

- Use questioning to seek out further information.
- Contribute ideas through using the imagination.
- Identify with characters and actions through role playing.
- Create and take part in improvised scenes.
- Gain confidence in their own abilities, particularly to communicate verbally and non-verbally.

Problems, emotions or challenges to be explored

- The main problem faced in this story surrounds the need for the boy to face his fears and make the long walk along the corridor to the safety of his grandmother's room. He has just experienced his first nightmare and, in a sense, understands something of the world he was previously oblivious to.

The session

The ideas presented are intended to be adapted and shaped by you for use in your class. They are not intended as a formula to follow or as a lesson plan. You may feel that you would like, for example, to take one idea and expand on it depending on the interests of your class or you may want to sequence a few of the ideas together. The text should help inspire teaching with a purpose which creates passion and empowers the class. This will depend, not only on the interests of your class, but also on your characteristics as a teacher. Some ideas will resonate more strongly with you than others. I hope the ideas you do use and embellish will mean that your class encounters imaginative teaching with purpose and passion for empowerment.

Connecting with the theme

Introduce the theme by discussing with the class whether they had a special item such as a toy or a blanket which, as they were growing up, they could not be separated from. You might be able to share your own item with the class (if you had such an item!) and tell them a story relating to its importance to you. Give the children time to remember and tell their own stories at this point. Ask the class whether they can remember why it was so special? Who made it or gave it to them? Can they remember what it was like to be apart from it? Have they still got it now?

Introducing the text

Introduce the text and tell the class that this story is about a boy who had his own very special blanket which was made by his grandmother. Look at the front cover with the class and identify the border of the front cover as the patchwork blanket. Open the book to the first page which shows the blanket in full. The class will be able to identify the sun, moon and stars. Ask the class to predict what they think the boy might use his cloth of dreams for? The class will also be able to identify the sun, moon and starts in the illustration accompanying the first page of text where we are told that the boy trips on his cloth of dreams and tears it.

As you read the text make links to the children's own lives. You may ask them whether they visit anyone special. What do they look forward to when they visit? Read to the point where his grandmother sees the holes and smiles sadly to herself before making her way to her room. Thought track the grandmother in order to discover what she might be thinking. You may want to recreate the scene in the class or you may prefer for the children to speak out her thoughts as you go round the class indicating the children you would like to say what they consider the grandmother would be thinking.

The first nightmare

We are told that this is the first time that the boy experiences nightmares. Invite the children, in groups, to think about one of the boy's dreams to depict as a freeze-frame. After a short discussion time invite the children to decide on a caption for their freeze-frame. Count down from five to zero, when the groups should freeze. Storytell the events of that night as the boy went to bed and the chain of nightmares came to him. Then go round the freeze-frames in turn asking groups to insert the caption of the freeze-frame into your narrative. For example you may say 'the first nightmare was a premonition of . . . followed by the anticipation of . . .' The aim is to build the freeze-frames into the narrative of the tale being told. Read the text describing the dreams the boy had and show the accompanying illustration.

The long walk

The boy wakes from his nightmares and finds himself on the floor. He knows that he needs to go to his grandmother's room so his cloth of dreams can be fixed. The text tells us that when he opens his bedroom door he sees how dark the walk will be. Use the drama convention of 'decision alley' which is also sometimes known as the 'thought tunnel' or 'conscience corridor' to give children the opportunity to voice the boy's thoughts. Invite children to form two lines facing each other in the classroom. Choose one child to take on the role of the boy. He will slowly walk down the corridor listening to the conflict in his own mind voiced by the children forming the lines. Once he has walked the corridor give him time to consider what he has heard and then decide on his course of action. It is important that you honour the decision the boy makes and so if, on balance, he decides to go back to his bed then you will need to weave this decision into the story. You could for example, before reading on, narrate 'as he climbed back into bed and pulled his blanket tightly around him he could not get the images of the nightmares out of his mind. He was scared to stay awake and scared to go to sleep. He now knew that he just had to make the long walk to his grandmother's room.'

Create the scene in the classroom of the 'long walk' from his bedroom to his grandmother's room. Talk with the class about what he might see, hear and feel as he makes his way along the landing. You could explore his emotions by using the idea from the game 'What's the time Mr Wolf?' The children who are going to make the walk will be at one end of the classroom. They will need to slowly make their way along the landing in the direction of the grandmother's room which is where a child will be facing away from the rest of the group. Tell the children that they should slowly and quietly make their way towards the safety of their grandmother's room but when the child turns round they should freeze as they will have heard, seen or felt something which stops them 'dead in their tracks'. While the children are frozen, thought track their ideas.

As you hear the responses you may want to model some thoughts for the children using similes or personification in order to make the thoughts, sights and feelings vivid for the listener. You may want to use these ideas as a stimulus for writing with the class.

Facing your fears

Read on to the point where the text describes how the boy reaches out into the night sky and collects the materials he needs in order to fix his cloth of dreams. Discuss with the class what they might need a similar cloth for. Is there anything they are worried about, afraid of or need courage to overcome? I have seen this idea used in a year 6 class when discussing the upcoming tests they were involved in and the teacher supporting the children with what they need in order to be successful. Once the children have decided what they would like their cloth to represent they can start to think about what 'ingredients' will be needed and what they will be for. They may, for example, want to weave courage, love, happiness, light, wisdom or warmth into their cloth. For some of the ideas the children may want to use the structure below but it is important that this does not become a writing straightjacket and instead is a scaffold and support for those phrases the children want to write in this style.

Into my cloth I will weave	As . . .	To . . .
Courage		
Warmth		
Love		

Concluding the drama

Continue reading to the end of the text and discuss the change which has occurred and what they perceive the meaning or moral of the story. You may want to use this as an opportunity for the children to make their own cloths in the style of 'the cloth of dreams' either through painting, mosaics or sewing.

*

BEFORE I WAKE UP . . . (2016, PRESTEL PUBLISHING) BY BRITTA TECKENTRUP

- **Possible writing opportunities**: Story mapping
- **Interactive strategies**: Collage, role play, storytelling
- **Age range**: 5–11

Introduction

We have probably all had that experience when the alarm goes off in the morning and you feel yourself being pulled away from the dreamworld in order to enter reality. Sometimes you may wish you could immerse yourself a bit longer in the dreamworld before waking. This is a beautiful story about that special time between the dreamworld and reality when we are taken on a dream journey full of rich imagining. In this story the little girl goes on a journey supported by the light of the moon down to the oceans, through the storm, into the wood and into the jungle. Throughout the journey she is accompanied and protected by a lion which gives her the courage to continue. This simple but uplifting story reassures children that they do not need to feel alone and that with the right support and friendships they can sometimes experience things until now unknown.

Teaching objectives

- Contribute ideas through using the imagination.
- Identify with characters and actions through role playing.
- Gain confidence in their own abilities, particularly to communicate verbally and non-verbally.
- Use a range of dramatic forms to express ideas and feelings.
- Use questioning to seek out further information.

Problems, emotions or challenges to be explored

- Exploring the dream world can be exciting as it is a place where fantasy can meet reality and normal rules do not always apply. This in itself can challenge children as they imagine what this space could be like.
- Through reading this book children may talk about various events in their lives which are personal to them. The personal nature brings emotion as well as possibly an incentive to share and talk about these times. These will need to be listened to on an individual basis.

The session

The ideas presented are intended to be adapted and shaped by you for use in your class. They are not intended as a formula to follow or as a lesson plan. You may feel that you would like, for example, to take one idea and expand on it depending on the interests of your class or you may want to sequence a few of the ideas together. The text should help inspire teaching with a purpose which creates passion and empowers the class. This will depend, not only on the interests of your class, but also on your characteristics as a teacher. Some ideas will resonate more strongly with you than others. I hope the ideas you do use and embellish will mean that your class encounters imaginative teaching with purpose and passion for empowerment.

Connecting with the theme

Ask the children what they were doing before they woke up this morning! Some children may be able to tell you they were dreaming. If so spend some time talking about the dreams they had. Are there any children who don't think that they dream? What do they think dreams are for? Do any children dream about school?

If possible (and true) share with the children a story about one of your dreams and how you did not want to be woken up from it. Explain that even though you heard the alarm clock going off you incorporated the sound into your dream in order to stay in the comfortable and secure world of your own imagination. Ask if any other children have experienced this feeling in the time between being asleep and being awake.

Introducing the text

Explain that you are going to read a story about this time called *Before I Wake Up* . . . Show the front cover and introduce the main character. Ask for predictions about the events which might take place. Open the book to the inside papers which show the girl in the forest surrounded by a range of animals. Does this picture support their predictions?

The illustrations by Britta Teckentrup are beautiful, using a range of shapes and colours in a collage-like appearance which draw the reader into each page of the text. Take time to explore the illustrations with the children. For example looking at the illustrations on the title page, children may notice the bed, supported by the moon, just outside the window while the girl sleeps soundly inside.

Where could your dreams take you?

Read the first page to the point where it says 'imagining worlds'. Ask the children where they would like their dreams to take them. Give the children time to talk with each other about their dreamworld. Ask the children questions to help them extend their ideas and describe their world focusing on the colours and shapes depicted.

Collect together a range of newspapers and magazines for the children to sift through. They should look for colours and pictures which depict their dreamworld. Children could work individually or in small groups creating a depiction of their dreamworld using the pictures, colours and shapes from the resources. Once completed ask the children to name their dreamworld.

Continue reading the text as we join the girl on her journey. As the girl and the lion float over the seas ask the children what they might point out to each other down below. Role play this for the children as teacher in role. Then invite the children, in role as the girl and the lion, to point out what they might see beneath them as they fly over the sea. Encourage a sense of awe and wonder as you spot things, possibly for the first time.

On the journey the girl and the lion also face some storms. Talk with the children about times when they may have been scared at night. Discuss what helped them. You could make a list of things the girl could try to make sure, if she encounters a storm again, she will be safe.

Read to the point where the girl is in the forest surrounded by trees. So far the girl and her lion have:

> Flown into the night
> Landed in a blue meadow
> Travelled over the seas
> Gone through some storms
> Sailed the seas
> Swam with whales
> Dived into the ocean
> Followed a path through the wood.

Imagining possibilities

Copy the illustrations for the children to explore in small groups. See if they can sequence the story as they remember it. Invite the children to retell parts of the story to each other as they share the pictures. You could model this to the children by picking a picture and retelling what happened to the girl and the lion. Then a child may pick a different picture and retell that event.

Introduce a blank page for the children. Ask them, in pairs, to imagine where the girl might go to next. Some children may follow the pattern in the story and imagine somewhere such as a mountainous region or the desert whereas others may think of locations which divert away from the pattern of the book such as going into space or arriving in a city. After children have talked about their idea give them time to draw their location and then, if appropriate, to write in the style of Britta Teckentrup a description of where they are.

Concluding the drama

Continue reading to the end of the story. You may want to use the illustrations to recap and retell the story with the children again. It would be useful to make the book available for the children to read for themselves. Laminating the illustrations and displaying them around the room and outside area will also stimulate conversations.

Ask the children where they would like to go in the dreams before they wake up. Remind the children that this is the special time in-between their deep sleep and them waking up – a time when special journeys can occur. Discuss with the children where your journey would take you. Explain to the children why you would want to go to each place and how you would get there. Then ask the children to share their own ideas for where they would like to go on their journey.

Using the story-mapping technique ask the children to draw their own journey. It should start with them in their bed, follow a sequence of around four locations before ending back in the bed before they wake up. Allow time for the children to draw, reflect, ponder and talk about their journey. Once each child has an outline of where their dream would take them, encourage the children to compare journeys and talk about them before moving into a more formal storytelling format.

*

LITERATURE LINKS RELATING TO THE THEME

There are many other books which explore the theme of this chapter. You may want to use them to complement the work you are doing or see how some of the drama strategies will enable you to enrich the learning experience. Suitable recommendations for use with process drama include:

Can I Play Too? (2010, Hyperion Books) by Mo Willems

How to Catch a Star (2015, Harper Collins Children's Books) by Oliver Jeffers

Ruby's Wish (2015, Chronicle Books) by Shirin Yim Bridges

Salt in His Shoes (2008, Aladdin Paperbacks) by Deloris Jordan

Wonder Goal! (2009, Anderson Press) by Michael Foreman

Matthew's Dream (2014, Anderson Press) by Leo Lionni.

14 Creative ideas with texts
Short stories

There are many short stories which can be used to create imaginative opportunities within the classroom. Short stories sometimes offer extended narrative which you can use to support the interactions you have with the text and can offer additional points for you to explore the problems, emotions and challenges through drama. The short stories chosen in this section are very different. The first is by the excellent author Shaun Tan who expertly creates gaps which the reader instinctively wants to fill. The second is by the established author Leon Garfield who, among other texts, writes some fantastic historical fiction. In both of these stories you will see how the authors create space leaving the reader to ask questions and use their imagination to solve the issues raised.

'STICK FIGURES' IN *TALES FROM OUTER SUBURBIA* (2009, TEMPLAR PUBLISHING) BY SHAUN TAN

- **Possible writing opportunities**: Debate, description of a scene, dialogue
- **Interactive strategies**: Freeze-frame, decision alley, role play, improvisation
- **Age range**: 7–11

Introduction

If you have not read *Tales from Outer Suburbia* by Shaun Tan I would highly recommend it to you. It is a collection of fifteen short stories illustrated superbly throughout. Each story will leave you with questions which are unanswered thereby compelling your inquisitive mind to try to fill in the gaps. 'Broken toys' for example leaves us wanting to know the relationship between the spaceman and the lady. When did they last see each other? Where had he been? Has he been injured? What is the significance of the broken toy? Other stories such as 'Distant Rain' and 'Why not make your own pet?' are beautifully presented offering a myriad of opportunities for imaginative engagement within the classroom.

The short story chosen for this section is 'Stick Figures'. It is a compelling mysterious story about stick figures which wander around a town, not speaking or showing emotion but just wandering. The people of the town are used to them and generally ignore them apart from the younger generation who seem to take pleasure in trying to destroy them only to see their bodies regenerated the next day from dead branches and their heads formed by clumps of turf. The drama leads us to try to solve some of the problems, emotions and challenges posed by the short story.

Teaching objectives

- Understand and take pleasure in the difference between pretence and reality.
- Identify with characters and actions through role playing.
- Realise that the views of individuals do not always coincide.
- Explore the differences between right and wrong in simple moral dilemmas posed through drama.
- Contribute ideas through using the imagination.
- Use a range of dramatic forms to express ideas and feelings.
- Use questioning to seek out further information.
- Create and take part in improvised scenes in order to explore particular issues which could, for instance, have a practical, social or moral dimension.

Problems, emotions or challenges to be explored

- The challenge in this text is how we deal with things that we do not understand or do not know how to communicate with. Parallels can easily be made with issues of friendship both in school and beyond.
- There is also an issue surrounding perceived progress as the town has been built seemingly with blatant disregard for the environment which was there before. When is it right to destroy wildlife for new buildings?
- One of the emotional connections the text brings is the need to understand what the stick men are thinking. It is not until the last page that there is an indication of what they may be thinking but as a reader there are gaps throughout the text for us to explore this.

The session

The ideas presented are intended to be adapted and shaped by you for use in your class. They are not intended as a formula to follow or as a lesson plan. You may feel that you would like, for example, to take one idea and expand on it depending on the interests of your class or you may want to sequence a few of the ideas together. The text should help inspire teaching with a purpose which creates passion and empowers the class. This will depend, not only on the interests of your class, but also on your characteristics as a teacher. Some ideas will resonate more strongly with you than others. I hope the ideas you do use and embellish will mean that your class encounters imaginative teaching with purpose and passion for empowerment.

Connecting with the theme

Share with the children something that irritates you, maybe the top being left off the toothpaste! Then ask the children to discuss the types of things which irritate them. You might want to unpick the word irritate first with the children so they know that we are talking about those little annoyances which we all encounter day to day which 'get under our skin' rather than some of the bigger issues which we may not like.

Share with the children how you have dealt with the issue that irritates you (buy toothpaste with a flip lid rather than one which comes off completely!) and then ask the children what action they have taken. This should be a playful time when you can have fun with the different irritations and share possible solutions.

Introducing the text

Show the illustration which is on the opposite page to the text. If possible provide each small group with a copy of the picture and give them time to share their initial thoughts before you structure their discussion. Encourage the children to talk about what they know from the picture, what they think from the picture and any questions which they want to find out after looking at the picture. Give an opportunity for children to join groups together to share their ideas before drawing the class together to discuss tends which are emerging. Pose the question to the children of what they think the story might be called.

First encounters

Read the first paragraph stopping to note some important clues within the text. Discuss what we find out about the stick men and how they are perceived by the humans. We read that when they are seen in the road people drive round them as if you would if they were 'a piece of cardboard or a dead cat'. This possibly indicates that the people see them as rubbish, lifeless and without worth. We also are told how the people try to keep them away from their houses. Discuss whether the children think that the stick men intentionally go towards the front of people's houses. If so what could their reasons be?

The last sentence of the first paragraph is significant. You may want to draw it to the children's attention now or return to it later in the story. We find out that stick men have always been in the area, 'since before anyone remembers, since before the bush was cleared and all the houses were built'. We can start to consider what their intentions could be. With the children generate questions to add to the ones posed in the initial discussions. You may want to also see if any of the previous questions can be answered.

At the end of the page we find out that children are told, by their parents, to leave the stick men alone but when the children question their parents for a reason why, the reasons are unclear. This is a great opportunity to explore what the reasons might be. Invite the children to form pairs. One will be in role as a parent and the other in role as a child. Storytell that the children had been playing with the stick men outside their houses. They were enjoying bringing out old clothes to dress them up. They even had a little competition going between them to see who could get the most clothes on a stick man before it collapsed from the weight. Continue to storytell that suddenly the front door opened and the child was called into the house. Reluctantly they went inside only to be told that they are never to play with the stick men again. This is the point where the role play will pick up from. The child should question their parent about the reasons why they should not play with the stick men; I mean after all, they aren't doing any harm – are they?

Once the children have had time to role play the scenario draw them back together and collect any reasons that have been given. Discuss the ones which lead to an air of mystery and that are in tune with the text. Build the role play by asking two pairs to form a group of four. Here you will have two parents and two children. You may want to storytell an introduction to the role play again but changing the scenario slightly from last time to give slightly different information. After a suitable amount of time draw the children back together and again discuss the reasons given.

Extending the drama

Continue reading to page 67. Here we find out that some people attack the stick men but get bored because of the way the stick men react – just standing there and taking it. Imagine with the children that the boys, after destroying a number of stick men have one left. It is just standing, staring – unflinching. Instead of destroying this stick man the boys encircle it discussing what they should do. Some think that they should continue to destroy all the stick men they see whereas others in the group are more inquisitive about them and want to try to find out more. Use the drama convention of the decision alley to explore the conflicting thoughts of the group at this time. Ask the children to form two lines facing each other. Choose another child to represent the group. They will need to walk down the alley hearing the thoughts of the group about what they should do with the stick man.

Alternatively you could ask the children to form a circle around a chair. The chair will represent the stick man and the children will be in role as members of the group who are discussing what they think they should do with the stick man. With yourself in the circle model how the convention works by stepping out, touching the chair and voicing what you think should happen to the stick man. Children will follow your lead and after a period of time you will have heard a range of opinions. Some will want to destroy the stick man, some may want to let it go back to wandering the streets whereas others may want to take it into their home.

Creating tension and conflicts

Read page 68 giving time for the children to consider who might be removing the earth from the lawns. These events are happening at night. Possibly this is a time of regeneration for the stick men. Explain that although people knew this went on no one had actually seen the events taking place at night and no one really knew the reasons why the stick men came back. However rumours and gossip were rife with snippets of information being shared as people queued for the bus or took their children to school. The snippets were just that – small pieces of information which, if pieced together, may reveal the secrets of the town but until then would remain simply snippets.

Share with the children a snippet you have heard about the events each night before inviting the children to start to walk around the classroom in role as the people from the town. They will each have a snippet of information to share. It might be something they saw, something they heard or something they have been told about the stick men at night. Whatever it is, when you clap your hands they should tell the person closest to them before continuing to walk. You may want to give the children three or four opportunities to share their snippet before bringing the class back together. Discuss as a whole group what we have learnt about the stick men so far. Look back at the questions generated at the start of the lesson. Ask which ones we have some information for and which still need answering. Maybe there will be more questions to add.

Concluding the drama

Read the last page and show the illustration. This is the only point in the story where we are given an indication of what the stick men might be thinking. Use the drama convention of forum theatre to recreate the picture in the classroom. Ask three children to come and represent the stick men standing on the hill staring down at the town. Discuss with the class what their interpretation is of the last page before inviting the children to come and voice the interior monologue of the stick men. This can be an interchangeable, free-flowing drama convention where children come and tap one of the stick men on the shoulder before voicing their thoughts. They would step back allowing another child to follow by tapping a stick man on the shoulder and voicing a thought or possibly posing a question.

Make this your own

You could recreate a secret meeting held by the stick men one night. Maybe they will be planning to take over the town and regain their land. I wonder how they would plan to do this. What would their strategy be? Children, working in small groups could role play the meeting and then make a plan for reclaiming the town.

*

FAIR'S FAIR (2008, WAYLAND) BY LEON GARFIELD

- **Possible writing opportunities**: Descriptive writing, diary, letter, newspaper recount
- **Interactive strategies**: Freeze-frame, hot seating, decision alley, improvisation
- **Age range**: 5–11

Introduction

Set in Victorian times *Fair's Fair* is a story about a boy called Jackson who sits on the same doorstep at the worst end of the worst street in the worst part of town. We meet him as he is eagerly waiting to eat the steaming pie he is holding in payment for a night's work. However a huge dog approaches and Jackson decides to give him half of his pie. In doing so Jackson sees a key around the dog's neck. Curiosity and the fact that he had nothing else to do meant that Jackson went with the dog as they tried door after door until one did finally open. Unknowingly Jackson is tested to see how honest he is before he finds out who has devised the challenges for him.

Teaching objectives

- Identify with characters and actions through role playing.
- Explore the differences between right and wrong in simple moral dilemmas posed through drama.
- Contribute ideas through using the imagination.
- Use a range of dramatic forms to express ideas and feelings.
- Use questioning to seek out further information.
- Create and take part in improvised scenes in order to explore particular issues which could, for instance, have a practical, social or moral dimension.

Problems, emotions or challenges to be explored

- We have an emotional connection with the main character in the story, a boy called Jackson. When reading we will instinctively want Jackson to be safe.
- We are concerned for Jackson's safety when he enters an old 'dead' house.
- There is a dilemma as Jackson comes across more food and wealth than he has ever seen before. The temptation may be to take advantage of this.

The session

The ideas presented are intended to be adapted and shaped by you for use in your class. They are not intended as a formula to follow or as a lesson plan. You may feel that you would like, for example, to take one idea and expand on it depending on the interests of your class or you may want to sequence a few of the ideas together. The text should help inspire teaching with a purpose which creates passion and empowers the class. This will depend, not only on the interests of your class, but also on your characteristics as a teacher. Some ideas will resonate more strongly with you than others. I hope the ideas you do use and embellish will mean that your class encounters imaginative teaching with purpose and passion for empowerment.

Introducing the text

Put the book into a clear plastic wallet and pretend there is a padlock on the zip. Explain to the class that you are unable to access the book until a range of clues have been found. Tell them that to find the code you need to know three things from each table. Ask each table to think of something they know about the text, something they think about the text and something that they wonder about the text in the form of one question. You may need to give each table a colour photocopy of the front and back cover of the book if you don't have enough for one per table group. Once the children have had time to look at the front and back cover ask each group to report back on something they know, think and wonder about the text. If possible collect these ideas together so you can refer back to them throughout the reading of the book. Explain that they have cracked the code and the padlock can be unlocked!

First encounters

The opening line of *Fair's Fair* is fantastic: 'Jackson was thin, small and ugly, and stank like a drain'. Discuss with the children whether they like the way the story starts. Does it encourage them to read on? Are they intrigued about Jackson? Continue reading the first page and discuss why Jackson would sit in the same place each day and why he would stay in the worst street in town. What could be the reason for him staying there?

You may want to create a role on the wall of Jackson as the text offers us a great deal of specific information which we know about him but also leaves questions for us to ponder. Draw round an outline of a child and display the role on the wall inviting children to add what they know about Jackson around the outside and questions they have about him inside. This can be added to throughout the story.

The second page is interesting. Read the first paragraph with the children. You could add questions to the role on the wall through your discussions. Note with the children the way that we are left to feel unsure about Jackson's past due to the word 'might'. Explore how that word influences the reader. You could try replacing it with other words. Does it have the same impact? At the end of the paragraph we are told that no one did miss Jackson when he disappeared and 'was never seen or heard of again'. This is an interesting phrase to use as it gives us an indication of what might happen to him in the story. Give the children time to discuss their predictions.

Continue reading the rest of the page where once again a single word holds a great deal of significance. 'It' in a way represents the whole story. 'It' happened. We know that Jackson was never seen or heard of again and the 'it' will hopefully fill in the gaps for us. In the same paragraph notice how the personification used helps us understand what the weather was like as Jackson sits on the doorstep.

On the next page we see Jackson sat on the doorstep. Use the drama convention of thought tracking to explore what he might be thinking as he sits clutching the pie. Maybe he will be reminiscing, maybe he will be imagining the taste of the pie or maybe he will be thinking about where he will sleep tonight. As you circulate around the classroom narrate this page of the story stopping every so often to capture one of Jackson's thoughts by tapping one of the children on the shoulder to indicate they should voice a thought.

Extending the drama

We soon find out that a huge dog approaches Jackson and tells Jackson, not in words but through his actions, that he is just as hungry. Jackson therefore shares his pie with the dog. Discuss with the children what this tells us about Jackson's character. After finding a key round the dog's neck Jackson sets off with the intention to take the dog home.

Read to the point where Jackson and the dog are on top of Hampstead Heath after walking through the snow trying the key in every house. At this point Jackson must be wondering whether it is worth carrying on. We are told that the dog begins to whine, snarl and growl. Something inside Jackson is telling him that the doorstep is a better place than this. Use the drama convention of decision alley to explore Jackson's thoughts. Should he continue to walk with the dog in search of what the key might open or should he return to his doorstep? Invite the children to form two lines facing each other in the classroom. Choose a child to represent Jackson who will walk down the alley hearing a range of views about what he should do. You may want to be part of the decision alley yourself in order to model a response which gives a point of view and also the reasoning behind it. You may say, for example, 'I should carry on because it can't just be by chance that the dog found me and had a key. Maybe, just maybe this will change my life'.

Once the child representing Jackson has walked through the alley ask the other children to sit down before hearing what Jackson's decision will be. You will need to honour the decision so if he decided to go back to the doorstep be prepared to storytell this part of the scenario. You could say that Jackson took the key, said goodbye to the dog and made his way back to the doorstep. However each day Jackson would hold the key, look at the key, wondering, until one day when the dog came back. You may want to use the drama convention of thought tracking here before returning to the text.

Jackson finally finds the house. Spend some time absorbing the delicious descriptive language which Leon Garfield uses. Discuss what we know about the house from the description. Jackson puts the key into the lock, opens the door and walks in. At this point you may want the children to stand up. Tell them to imagine that they are stood in the hallway to the house. They should think about their senses and be ready to voice something they see, hear, smell, touch, taste or feel. Once again you may want to model some of the responses saying 'I can see shadows dancing formed by the flickering of the candle flame', 'I can hear the faint laughter of the house deep in its belly knowing that it has lured me in', 'I feel alone – all alone'. As you describe this moment for Jackson circulate around the classroom occasionally tapping children on the shoulder to indicate that they should voice their sense at this point.

After hearing a range of senses invite the children, in small groups, to create a sense splat. You can do this in a number of ways. You may want to give each group a piece of flipchart paper for them to note down Jackson's response to each of the senses, or you may want to display each individual sense around the classroom and the children to use sticky notes on their tables before putting them on the appropriate sense. Encourage children to use phrases rather than single words as the phrases will support their writing activity. Again you may need to model this, showing how you want to say that Jackson is scared and could write the word scared down but in order to use it in your writing you want to turn it into a phrase. You may write therefore 'Jackson stood still, unable to move, unable, for a moment, to breath . . .'.

You could use the ideas as a writing opportunity to describe the moment when Jackson walked into the house. This will support children in knowing that you do not need to have lots of action taking place, indeed Jackson could stand in the same place for the duration of the descriptive piece. The writer is taking the reader into the hallway and describing what can be seen and heard but the writer will also know whether they want to make the reader feel concerned for Jackson.

Once you have shared the stories from the children return to the text and read to the point where Jackson and Lillipot are telling each other what their names are. Discuss with the children what they think is happening. Who do they think is behind the events? Are they watching what is happening and what are their intentions? You may also want to discuss the issue of temptation. There is possibly more food and wealth in the house than either child has seen before. Do the children think they would be tempted to take advantage of it? What does this tell us about the character of Jackson and Lillipot?

Read on to where Jackson and Lillipot fall asleep in front of the fire. Tell the children that Jackson starts to dream. His dreams are of his life before he found the dog as he remembers sitting on the doorstep, scrubbing the floors, running errands and holding horses. In his dream he remembers one desperate day when he was sat on the doorstep cold and hungry with seemingly no hope in his life. Jackson wishes he could call to himself in the dream and tell him that everything will be OK. He tries and calls out some reassuring words. Use the drama convention of thought tracking to explore what Jackson might say to himself.

Further on in the text, after Jackson and Lillipot have given their mince pies to the carol singers two men confront them. Read to the point where one man says 'We'll take it all'. Ask the children to get into groups of four. Two will represent the men and the other two will represent Jackson and Lillipot. The men want to steal from the house whereas Jackson and Lillipot want to convince them not to. Role play the discussion stopping occasionally to explore the points being raised. Through the discussion you may find the children having a deeper understanding of the character of Jackson and Lillipot.

Read on to the end of the story where the men reveal themselves and Jackson and Lillipot find out that they can stay in the house forever. Ask the children what they feel the message of the story is. Tell the children that that evening Lillipot, Jackson and Mr Beecham Chambers sat down for their first meal together but they all had so many questions for each other. Use the drama convention of hot seating to find out more about the three characters. Children should be in role as Jackson, Lillipot and Mr Beecham Chambers and be prepared to answer questions from the rest of the children.

Make this your own

Imagine that people did miss Jackson and Lillipot as they always used to turn up to do their errands regardless of illness, weather or tiredness. So as the weeks went by, without any sign of the two children, some people did get worried. Invite the class to produce missing posters for Jackson and Lillipot. Discuss what the features would be and use the text to find the information needed for the poster.

Imagine that in a few years' time once Jackson and Lillipot were truly settled in their new way of life a reporter got to hear about the story. Invite children to write the rags to riches story with interviews with Jackson, Lillipot and Mr Beecham Chambers.

*

LITERATURE LINKS RELATING TO THE THEME

There are many other books which explore the theme of this chapter. You may want to use them to complement the work you are doing or see how some of the drama strategies will enable you to enrich the learning experience. Suitable recommendations for use with process drama include:

The Rope and Other Stories (2000, Puffin) by Philippa Pearce

Sky Ship and Other Stories (2004, A and C Black) by Geraldine McCaughrean

The Bent Back Bridge (1999, Franklin Watts) by Gary Crew

How the Whale Became and Other Stories (1963, Faber and Faber) by Ted Hughes

The Swap and Other Stories (1997, Macmillan) by George Layton

Once Upon an Alphabet (2014, Harper Collins Children's Books) by Oliver Jeffers

M Is for Magic (2008, Bloomsbury Publishing PLC) by Neil Gaiman

Shakespeare's Stories for Young Readers (2012, Dover Publications) by E. Nesbit.

Index